Better Homes and Gardens®

gifts to make

a simply handmade™ book

365 beautifully easy ideas

Better Homes and Gardens® Books
Des Moines, Iowa

Better Homes and Gardens® Books
A Simply Handmade™ Book

gifts to make: 365 beautifully easy ideas

Editor: Carol Field Dahlstrom
Contributing Writer: Susan M. Banker
Graphic Designer: Marisa Dirks
Contributing Designer: Tim Abramowitz
Copy Chief: Terri Fredrickson
Copy and Production Editor: Victoria Forlini
Editorial Operations Manager: Karen Schirm
Managers, Book Production: Pam Kvitne, Marjorie J. Schenkelberg
Contributing Copy Editor: Arianna McKinney
Contributing Proofreaders: Judy Friedman, Colleen Johnson, Elise Marton
Photographers: Andy Lyons Cameraworks, Pete Krumhardt, Scott Little
Technical Illustrator: Chris Neubauer Graphics, Inc.
Electronic Production Coordinator: Paula Forest
Editorial and Design Assistants: Kaye Chabot, Mary Lee Gavin,
Karen McFadden

Meredith® Books
Editor in Chief: James D. Blume
Design Director: Matt Strelecki
Managing Editor: Gregory H. Kayko

Director, Sales, Special Markets: Rita McMullen
Director, Sales, Premiums: Michael A. Peterson
Director, Sales, Retail: Tom Wierzbicki
Director, Book Marketing: Brad Elmitt
Director, Operations: George A. Susral
Director, Production: Douglas M. Johnston

Vice President and General Manager: Douglas J. Guendel

Better Homes and Gardens Magazine
Editor in Chief: Karol DeWulf Nickel

Meredith Publishing Group
President, Publishing Group: Stephen M. Lacy
Vice President-Publishing Director: Bob Mate

Meredith Corporation
Chairman and Chief Executive Officer: William T. Kerr

Chairman of the Executive Committee: E. T. Meredith III

All of us at Better Homes and Gardens® Books are dedicated to providing you with information and ideas to create beautiful and useful projects. We welcome your comments and suggestions. Write to us at: Better Homes and Gardens Books, Crafts Editorial Department, 1716 Locust Street, LN 112, Des Moines, IA 50309-3023.

Permission is granted to photocopy patterns for personal use only.

If you would like to purchase any of our books, check wherever quality books are sold. Visit our website at bhg.com

simply handmade

Our lives are graced by the people who bring meaning to it. We have friends who know us better than we know ourselves—and love us anyway. There are relatives who make us laugh, and those who give the best hugs. There are neighbors, teachers, and acquaintances who, for a million reasons, make their way into our lives and hearts.

To celebrate all of those special relationships that we cherish, this book shares hundreds of handcrafted gift ideas that say, "you mean the world to me." Whether you want to acknowledge a birthday, a holiday, a housewarming, an anniversary, or just want to remember a dear friend, you'll be delighted with these doable, yet spectacular projects.

Try your hand at painting sparkling glass candlesticks or stenciling a backyard rock. Challenge your creativity with a new technique, such as soapmaking, sewing, ribbon weaving, or etching. Scoop up last-minute gift wrap ideas that are simply unforgettable.

When you're searching for that perfect present for the people you adore, let them know how special they are to you with a meaningful gift you craft yourself. And don't forget clever wrapping, which is as wonderful as the surprise inside.

Happy gift-giving!

Carol Field Dahlstrom

contents

4

between friends

■ Friendship, one of the most cherished blessings in life, is the focus in this fun-to-make gift section. Craft candles, place mats, flowerpots, soap—all kinds of wonderful things to share your talent and affection with all your best friends.

very special occasions

■ Whether you want to honor a newborn, newlyweds, or new neighbors, this chapter offers delightful projects to make and give with pride.

clever wraps & bows

□ Top off wrapped gifts with colorful bows that are as special as the surprises inside. Learn bow basics that are sure to add package pizzazz.

about this book

Use your time and talent to make gifts for everyone dear to your heart. Make holidays, anniversaries, and housewarmings unforgettable. Surprise special friends with handmade treasures and find new ways to say *Happy Birthday.* This book offers a glorious selection of projects to make and give for every occasion. To help you plan your crafting time, the projects are categorized into three levels:

When you're short on time ...

good ideas candied flowerpots

Hard candies transform ordinary terra-cotta pots into cheerful holiday servers. Simply hot-glue the candies around the rim of a pot and let cool. Fill the pot with sweets of the season. Place a votive candle in a cup for a last-minute holiday gift.

... look for a Good Ideas project. While they may be last-minute, these gifts are loaded with appeal.

Craft beautiful handmade gifts and wraps that celebrate all

peacock feather plate
make it in minutes

Share the breathtaking colors of a peacock feather by decoupaging it on a clear glass plate.

to make this plate you'll need:
Clear glass plate with smooth bottom
Peacock feather
Scissors
Decoupage medium
Paintbrush
Purchased small chocolate candies

present*ations*

here's how
To make this project, wash and dry the plate thoroughly. Turn the plate over. Position the peacock feather on the plate and cut edges to fit. Remove the feather. Paint a layer of decoupage medium onto the back of the plate. Reposition the feather, adhering it to the plate. Carefully paint another layer of decoupage medium over the feather. Allow the plate to dry. Trim any edges of the feather that extend beyond the plate edge. Arrange candy on the plate.

I more idea...
Decoupage an assortment of pretty feathers on the outside of a clear glass vase.

For a coordinating wrap, place the plate in a box lined with shredded paper. Wrap the box with teal paper. Tie variegated ribbon across the middle of the box. Tuck two feathers under the ribbon. Add a gift tag if desired.

to make this wrap you'll need:
Box
Shredded paper
Teal wrapping paper
Variegated ribbon
Scissor
Peacock feather

Sprinkled throughout the book you'll find PRESENTATIONS —glorious gift wrap ideas that shine with festive flair!

also try this...
Before placing the feather in the decoupage medium, comb it with a baby comb to smooth it out.

dressy

... choose something wonderful with a Make It in Minutes label. These projects will only take a little longer to accomplish, but the kudos are well worth it.

7

dainty decanters
step-by-step

Whether you fill these pretty vessels with wine or bath crystals, they're sure to be appreciated.

to make a decanter you'll need:
Clear glass decanter
Gloss paints in desired colors
Round toothpick
Pencil with round eraser
Paintbrush

▪ **Wash the decanter** and let dry. Avoid touching the areas to be painted.

▪ **To paint small flowers or dots,** dip a toothpick into paint and dot in a circle around the surface of the decanter. Let dry. Dot flower centers in a contrasting color if desired. Let dry.

▪ **To paint large flowers or dots,** dip a pencil eraser into paint and dot in a circle around the decanter. Let dry. Dot flower centers in a contrasting color

▪ **Continue painting flowers,** forming a line or scallop on the decanter. Add green leaves, dots, and swirls as desired. Let dry.

▪ **Bake the decanter** in the oven as instructed by the paint manufacturer. Cool and remove from oven.

I more idea...
Paint a set of matching wine glasses using this easy-to-paint technique.

also try this...
Paint an initial or monogram on a decanter and surround it with a floral motif.

pampering

... try a Step-by-Step project. These wondrous gifts are accompanied by how-to photographs so you can master a new technique with ease.

happy, happy birthday gifts

When someone is dear to your heart, send happy birthday wishes with a handmade gift you create with love. This colorful chapter offers a wonderful assortment of creative projects for you to make. Each of these birthday surprises is filled with the spirit of celebration and will remind your dear friends and relatives that they mean the world to you.

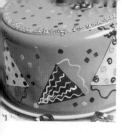

party hat cake carrier

make it in minutes

to make the
cake carrier
you'll need:
Screwdriver
Metal cake carrier
Newspapers
Spray primer
Aqua spray paint
Tracing paper
Pencil; toothpick
Scissors
Medium-weight
  cardboard
Acrylic enamel
  paints in yellow,
  white, red, green,
  bright pink, and
  blue
Paintbrushes,
  including a small
  flat brush
White paint marker
Black permanent
  fine-line marker

Perfect for toting birthday treats, this vintage cake cover enjoys a fresh start with lively painted designs.

hat pattern

here's how

To make this project, remove the knob from the cake carrier dome using a screwdriver, if necessary. Wash and dry the dome and the plate. To protect the center of the cake carrier plate from paint, tape a paper plate in the center of the carrier plate.

In a well-ventilated work area, cover the work surface with newspapers. Spray primer on the exterior of the dome and the rim of the plate. Let dry. Spray aqua paint over the primed areas. Let dry. Spray on a second coat. Let dry. Remove the paper plate.

Trace the hat pattern, *above*. Cut out the shape. Trace the pattern onto cardboard. Cut out.

Trace around the pattern several times on the sides of the dome, randomly turning the pattern.

To paint the hats, fill in each triangle with a solid color. Let dry. Paint lines,

dots, or other desired patterns on the triangles. To paint dots, dip a pencil eraser, a paintbrush handle, or round toothpicks into paint, and dot onto the surface. Paint wavy lines for the hat straps. Let dry.

To paint confetti, use a small flat paintbrush and a variety of paints. Dip the paintbrush into paint, and use small strokes to make little squares on the cake dome sides and top.

Using a white paint marker, write "happy birthday to you" several times around the top edge of the dome. Let dry. To make the lettering stand out, add black marker shadows on the left and bottom sides of each letter. Let dry, and replace the knob.

1 more idea...

Try this same idea on a clear glass cake server, substituting glass paints for acrylic enamels.

also try this...

Carry out the party-hat theme by painting the same motifs on a solid-color tablecloth using fabric paints.

celebrate

good ideas pastel wishes

Sparkling rock candy adds an unexpected touch to this candle display. Set a chunky candle in the center of a clear crystal dish. Arrange rock candy around the candle. Place a ribbon bow to one side of the candle. Light the candle as you sing, "Happy Birthday."

coffee talk

stickers on display

make it in minutes

Some stickers are so stylish,
 they deserve to be framed all by themselves.

here's how

To make this project, cut around desired stickers without removing the backing. Arrange the stickers on the mat or on a piece of heavyweight white cardboard to be framed. When the desired look is achieved, peel off each sticker backing and press into place. Layer the mat over the cardboard and insert the pieces into the frame.

15

1 more idea...

Decoupage phrases or headlines from newspapers or magazines for a newsworthy effect.

also try this...

Mount attractive postage stamps instead of stickers.

ribboned

woven ribbon purse

make it in minutes

Gather ribbons in muted colors and weave them together to make a small purse.

here's how

To make this project, mark off an 8½x17-inch rectangle centered on fusible interfacing. Pin the interfacing with the fusible side up.

Cut and pin an odd number of ribbons vertically on rectangle, allowing 1 inch of ribbon at each end. Weave ribbons horizontally starting at the lower edge of rectangle. Continue weaving and pinning ends until the rectangle is covered.

Trim top corners to make flap. Fuse ribbons to interfacing using a press cloth. Layer ribbon weaving to the wrong side of lining. Using the photo, opposite, as a guide, make a tracing paper pattern of bag approximately 6½x9 inches for the finished size. Cut out the pattern. Place pattern over weaving. Stitch around outside edge to secure ribbons to lining. Cut out close to stitching. Bind and stitch the bottom edge of the rectangle with the ⅝-inch rose ribbon, encasing weaving and lining. Fold up 6 inches and topstitch side seams. Bind and sew side seams and flap with rose ribbon.

Sew on closure. For large ribbon circle, cut a 6-inch length of 1-inch-wide ribbon. Seam the ends. Run a gathering stitch along one edge. Pull tightly; knot. Sew to bag. Attach button. For small ribbon circle, cut a 4½-inch length of ⅝-inch-wide ribbon. Repeat as for the large circle.

presentation

To wrap the purse, place it in a box and wrap with paper. Tie the package with curling ribbon. Tuck a rose under the ribbon. For the tag, cut two paper rectangles, one ¼ inch larger than the other. Trim the larger piece with decorative-edge scissors. Glue the small piece of paper atop the large piece. Using glitter glue, draw scallops around the edge of the small paper. Add a sticker and the words "Happy Birthday."

to make the purse you'll need:

Fabric marking pen
T-pins
10½x19-inch piece each of nonwoven fusible interfacing and lining
Scissors
6 different grosgrain ribbons in gray, rose, lavender, and taupe in ⅝-, 1-, and 1½-inch widths
Tracing paper
Press cloth
4 yards of ⅝-inch-wide rose-colored ribbon for edge
Thread
Needle
Snap or hook-and-loop closure
Ceramic buttons for trim

to make the gift wrap you'll need:

Box
Desired wrapping paper
Curling ribbon
Scissors
Rose
2 plain papers to coordinate with wrap
Decorative-edge scissors
Glue stick
Glitter glue
Glitter sticker
Metallic marker

1 more idea...
Weave ribbons to make a case for eyeglasses.

also try this...
Use bright ribbons to make a purse for a little girl.

Happy Birthday

sentimental

letters in lace

step-by-step

Pretty notepaper is always welcome, and this
lacy version comes in its own lovely folder.

to make the
notepaper and
folder you'll
need:
Large piece of
  textured white
  paper
Large piece of
  pastel paper
Scissors
Spray adhesive
Hot-glue gun
Hot-glue sticks
Watercolors
Paintbrush
White Rub 'n Buff
Assorted pastel
  papers
Braided trim and
  pearl trim
White tube-style
  paint
Ribbon

19

1 **To make the folder,** cut a piece of textured
paper approximately 13x22 inches. Fold each
edge under ⅝ inch. Clip corners to enable easier
folding.

2 **Cut a piece of pastel paper** to fit inside
the folded edges. In a well-ventilated work area,
spray adhesive on the back of the paper and
adhere to the inside of the folder.

3 **Lay the paper right side down;**
measure and mark 4½ inches from one end. Fold
on line to make a pocket. Hot-glue at edges to
secure. Hot-glue braided trim along edges where
decorative paper is folded over pastel paper. Fold
paper in half to make an envelope.

4 **For cards, cut and fold textured paper**
into a card. If the pattern on the paper permits, cut
the design along one edge and place over a solid
paper. Paint pastel sections of paper. Let dry. Apply
a coat of white Rub 'n Buff over raised areas on
card. Create additional cards and stationery using
pastel papers. Trim with cutout motifs from textured
paper, braided and pearl trim, and white paint.
Insert the cards into the folder and tie with ribbon.

1 more idea...
When making large quantities of note
cards, use white textured wallpaper.

also try this...
Sew beads onto areas of the paper
motif to add texture and interest.

pretty ice pail
make it in minutes

to make the ice pail you'll need:

Lightweight cardboard
Pencil
Ruler
Scissors
Metal pail approximately 8 inches high
Enamel paints in green, red, and turquoise
Paintbrush
White paint marker
Metal scoop
Ribbons

20

Paint a pail and fill it with ice and your favorite bottled drinks to spice up a birthday bash.

here's how

To make this project, cut a triangle pattern from the cardboard for the brim design. Trace it several times around the pail top, overlapping as shown in the photograph, *opposite,* to appear as layered cloths.

Paint the triangles, alternating the colors. Paint a turquoise stripe around the pail bottom. Let dry. Add a thin green line at the top of the turquoise. Add red dots above the turquoise stripe. Let dry. Add cream dotted lines at the edges of each triangle. Paint coordinating stripes on the scoop handle. Let dry. Add cream dots between the stripes. Let dry. Tie a multi-ribbon bow around the pail handle. Trim the ribbon ends if needed.

1 more idea...
Use metallic paints for a shimmery look.

also try this...
Paint tiny motifs on the blocks of color to resemble calico fabric.

cool reception

man in the moon plate
step-by-step

Tracing paper
Pencil
Tape
Large clear-glass
  plate
White glass paint
Small round brush
Craft paper
Scissors
White pearl spray
  paint
Light-colored easel

22

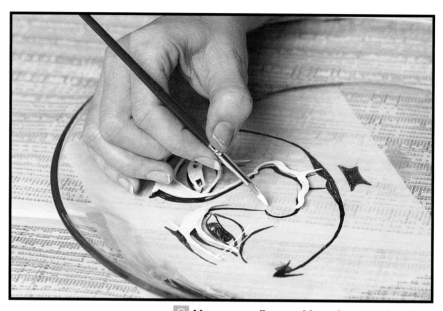

1 Trace the moon face pattern, *page 25,* onto tracing paper. Tape the pattern in place on the back side of the plate.

2 Use a small round brush and white glass paint to paint the face details, following the pattern from the other side. Let dry.

3 To make circle stencils, cut 1- and 1½-inch circles from a piece of craft paper. Place stencil on plate and sponge white paint over stencil randomly around face.

4 Lightly spray two or three even coats of white pearl paint over the painted face. Spray just enough to cover evenly but preserve translucency. Let dry.

5 Remove pattern. Place plate easel with a light source behind it.

Wrap instructions begin on page 24.

just heavenly

The perfect gift for the lighthearted, this quick-paint character is loaded with personality.

man in the moon plate (continued)

to wrap a plate you'll need:
Box with tissue
    paper
Blue wrapping
    paper
Tape
2-inch-wide sheer
    white ribbon
Scissors
5 white votive
    candles
White tulle
White heavy paper
Paper punch
Silver cord

24

presentation

To wrap this gift, cover a box with blue paper and tie with ribbon. Wrap votives in a length of tulle. Tie ends with ribbon. Cut a crescent shape from white paper. Punch a hole in one tip. Thread cord through hole and attach to ribbon.

Present a Man in the Moon Plate in an enlightening wrap—
with candles in tulle as a topper and a crescent moon tag.

1 more idea...
Paint the man in the moon on a round
glass tabletop for a real showpiece.

also try this...
Enlarge the pattern, *opposite*,
to paint a smiling moon on a
little one's wall.

Man in the Moon Plate Pattern

good ideas goodies in glass

When an ordinary candy dish just won't do, try layering colorful candies in a tall glass vase. Here, colorful jelly beans in all the birthday guy's or gal's favorite flavors add a sweet touch. Simply cover the top of the vase with clear cellophane and tie with bright curling ribbons. Or give some swirled candy sticks standing up in a vintage tumbler. For the presentation, just add a ribbon and a smile.

door plates

make it in minutes

to make a plate you'll need:
Ceramic plate with plain center
Grease pencil
Fine-point paint markers for glass and ceramic
Tracing paper and pencil, optional
Transfer paper, optional
Plate hanger

Personalize a space in your home with a designer-look plate.

here's how

To make this project, wash plate with soap and water; dry. Use a grease pencil to lightly write the desired word across the plate. Or trace one of the patterns, *pages 30–31,* and transfer to plate.

Use a paint marker to draw over the lines. Let the paint dry.

Attach a plate hanger to the plate and hang on door.

Gift wrap instructions are on page 30.

1 more idea...
Write a brief quote or favorite saying on a plate.

also try this...
Make four interchangeable seasonal plates to greet guests at the front door.

in the works

Studio

door plates (continued)

Studio

Studio Plate Pattern

presentation

to wrap a plate you'll need:

Two plastic foam disks, such as Styrofoam, slightly larger than the plate

Tape

Cellophane or tissue paper

Ribbon

Two scraps of colored paper

Scissors

Decorative-edge scissors

Glue stick

To wrap a plate, sandwich the plate between foam disks. Tape the disks together so they don't shift. Place on large square of cellophane or tissue paper. Gather at the top and secure with a ribbon bow.

Cut a two-layer tag from paper. Glue the smaller piece atop the larger one. Write a birthday message on the tag. Add a party noisemaker if desired.

Kitchen Plate Pattern

Office Plate Pattern

memento

Capture natural leaf shapes
to enjoy indoors with this
spray-painted photo frame.

fern frame

step-by-step

1 In a well-ventilated work area, cover the work surface with newspapers. Disassemble the frame. Spray the frame gold. Let dry. Apply a second coat if needed. Let dry.

2 Apply spray mount to the back sides of small sections of leaves. Arrange over the frame, overlapping as desired.

3 Spray random sections of the frame green. Spray the remaining areas blue, overlapping green slightly. Let the paint dry.

4 Carefully peel off the leaves. Reassemble the frame.

to make the frame you'll need:
Newspapers
Wide purchased picture frame
Gold metallic spray paint
Spray mount
Transparent glass spray paint in blue and green
Flat pressed fernlike leaves

presentation

To wrap this gift, photocopy family photographs and use the paper as wrap. Tape several copies together to make a large sheet. Tie package with a ribbon bow. Cut a tag using decorative-edge scissors.

to make the wrap you'll need:
Photocopies of old family photographs
Tape
Ribbon
Medium-weight paper
Decorative-edge scissors

1 more idea...
Use this technique to embellish flowerpots, lunch boxes, and furniture.

also try this...
Experiment with other leaf shapes, grasses, and weeds.

good ideas buckled bouquets

Vintage belt buckles add old-fashioned charm to these clever flower containers. Use ribbon to tie the buckles to straw bags or hats. Be sure to use a plastic liner before setting the plant or flowers inside.

dainty decanters
step-by-step

Whether you fill these pretty vessels with wine or bath crystals, they're sure to be appreciated.

to make a decanter you'll need:
Clear glass decanter
Glass paints in desired colors
Paintbrush
Pencil with round eraser

1 Wash the decanter and let dry. Avoid touching the areas to be painted.

2 To paint small flowers or dots, dip the handle of a paintbrush into paint and dot in a circle around the surface of the decanter. Let dry. Dot flower centers in a contrasting color if desired. Let dry.

3 To paint large flowers or dots, dip a pencil eraser into paint and dot in a circle around the decanter. Let dry. Dot flower centers in a contrasting color if desired. Let dry.

4 Continue painting flowers, forming a line or scallop on the decanter. Add green leaves, dots, and swirls as desired. Let dry.

5 Bake the decanter in the oven as instructed by the paint manufacturer. Cool and remove from oven.

1 more idea...
Paint a set of matching wine glasses using this easy-to-paint technique.

also try this...
Paint an initial or monogram on a decanter and surround it with a floral motif.

pampering

contain

mending jars

make it in minutes

Not just for jelly, these petite canning jars are cleverly transformed into handy organizers. Filled with sewing notions, they're the perfect birthday gift for a seamstress or mender.

to make a jar you'll need:
Pencil
4-ounce canning jar with lid and band
3x3-inch piece of 1-inch-thick foam
Scissors
Thread and needle
5-inch circle of calico fabric
2x2-inch piece of felt
Pinking shears
Thick white crafts glue
2¼x1¼-inch piece of card stock
Felt scraps
Items to fill jar, such as buttons, needles, thread, thimble, safety pins, etc.
18 inches of ⅛-inch-wide satin ribbon
Sew-through button
½-inch gold sewing charm

here's how

To make this project, trace the widest part of the band circle onto foam; cut out. Using thread, gather the outside edge of the calico circle. Place the circle of foam onto the top of the lid. Add the calico circle, pulling the gathers tight on the underside and allowing a ¾-inch opening.

Cut a 1½-inch circle of felt with pinking shears. Glue the felt over the gathered fabric on the underside of the lid. Smooth calico over the foam, pushing the foam away slightly at the lid edge. Add the band.

To make the thread and needle holder, cut card stock paper on the long sides using pinking shears. On one short side, stitch a piece of felt that is pinked on all sides and slightly larger than the card stock. Allow ⅜ inch of felt to fold over the end of the card stock.

Machine-stitch across one end of the felt, securing the card stock.

Wrap an assortment of thread around the card stock. Add safety pins at the stitched edge. Insert two needles under the thread into stitched edge.

Fill the jar with desired sewing notions. Tie the ribbon around the jar rim. Thread a button and a gold charm onto the ribbon. Tie the ribbon ends into a bow.

1 more idea...

Use holiday fabric when giving mending jars as stocking stuffers.

also try this...

For the crafter, fill a larger canning jar with assorted crafts supplies.

foresight

snazzy spec cases
make it in minutes

With a rainbow of felt and embroidery colors available, you can make personalized eyeglass cases to tuck into every birthday card.

to make
a case
you'll need:
Pencil
Tracing paper
Scissors
Felt in desired
  colors
Pins
Embroidery floss in
  desired colors

here's how

To make this project, trace the pattern, *pages 42-43,* for the desired eyeglasses case onto tracing paper. Cut out the pattern. Cut the pieces from felt colors of choice (these cases use black, fuchsia, blue, purple, and red).

For the bow case, lay the largest felt rectangle flat. Pin the smaller strip atop it as shown, *page 42.* Using three plies of floss, sew the two pieces together at the edges. Fold the case in half with right sides out. Sew the sides closed using three plies of floss and blanket stitches. To add French knot (see *page 43*) dots to the small bow shape, use six plies of desired colors of embroidery floss. Sew to the larger bow shape using blanket stitches. Wrap the center of the bow with embroidery floss. Tack the bow to the top of the eyeglasses case.

For the diamond case, sew the circle to the center of the diamond using blanket stitches (see *page 43*) and embroidery floss. Sew the diamond to its background shape using blanket stitches, centering it on one half of the felt piece. Pin felt piece to the remaining large background piece, and sew together using blanket stitches. Use embroidery floss to wrap the corner where the case meets the bow.

Patterns are on pages 42–43.

41

1 more idea...
Use simple quilt block or cookie cutter shapes for other case designs.

also try this...
Sew small buttons on the case to add three-dimensional polka dots.

snazzy spec cases (continued)

fold

bow case pattern

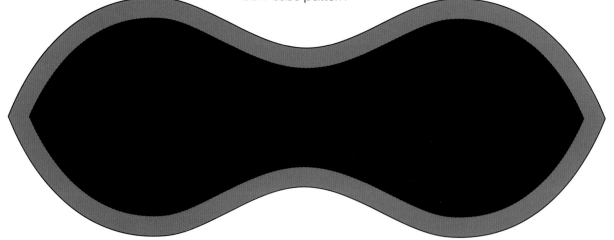

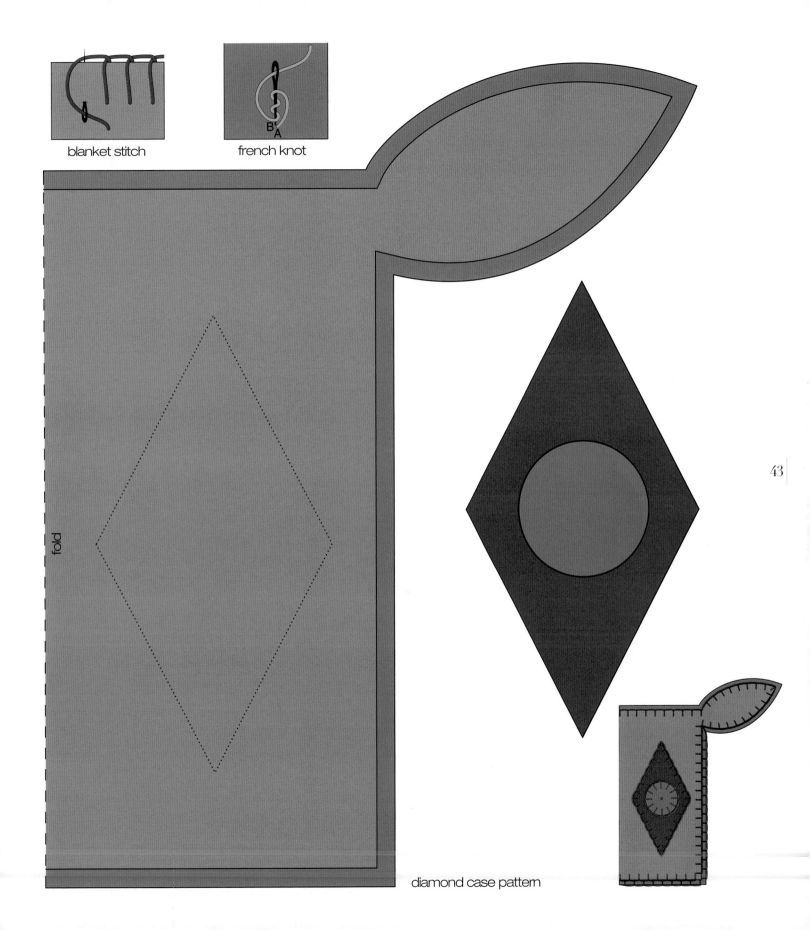

blanket stitch

french knot

fold

diamond case pattern

43

holiday gifts
year-round

■ As you await each holiday, think of it as an opportunity to remember the people in your life who bring you joy every day of the year. Whether it's a Halloween surprise, an Easter gift, or a special package to place beneath the Christmas tree, you'll find a bundle of creative treasures to make and give in this inspiring chapter.

"boo-tiful"

halloween tray

make it in minutes

here's how

To make a tray, remove the back and the glass. Cover the work surface with newspapers in a well-ventilated work area. Spray-paint the tray black. Let dry. Sand the edges for a worn appearance. Wipe away the dust using a tack cloth.

Arrange the photocopies as desired in the bottom of the tray, trimming the pieces as necessary to fit. Glue the paper pieces in place. Glue additional decorations, such as the tops from cupcake trims, in place. Let dry.

Clean the glass, and reassemble the tray.

Serving tray with glass insert and removable back
Newspapers
Black spray paint
Sandpaper
Tack cloth
Originals or color photocopies of Halloween postcards, sheet music, cupcake trims, napkins, magazine covers, greeting cards, or other desired items that are relatively flat
Thick white crafts glue

47

Share this Halloween tray with someone who loves to serve ghoulish concoctions.

1 more idea...
Add orange polka dots by dotting the tray with fingernail polish.

also try this...
Use Halloween stickers instead of cupcake trims for an all-flat version.

good ideas glitter-topped pumpkins

Miniature pumpkins make a big impression when embellished with glitter in Halloween colors. Use thick white crafts glue to draw designs on the pumpkin tops. Then sprinkle with glitter and shake off the excess. Present the little gems on a small silver platter with a glitter tag and you'll have made the perfect gift for the next monstrous gathering.

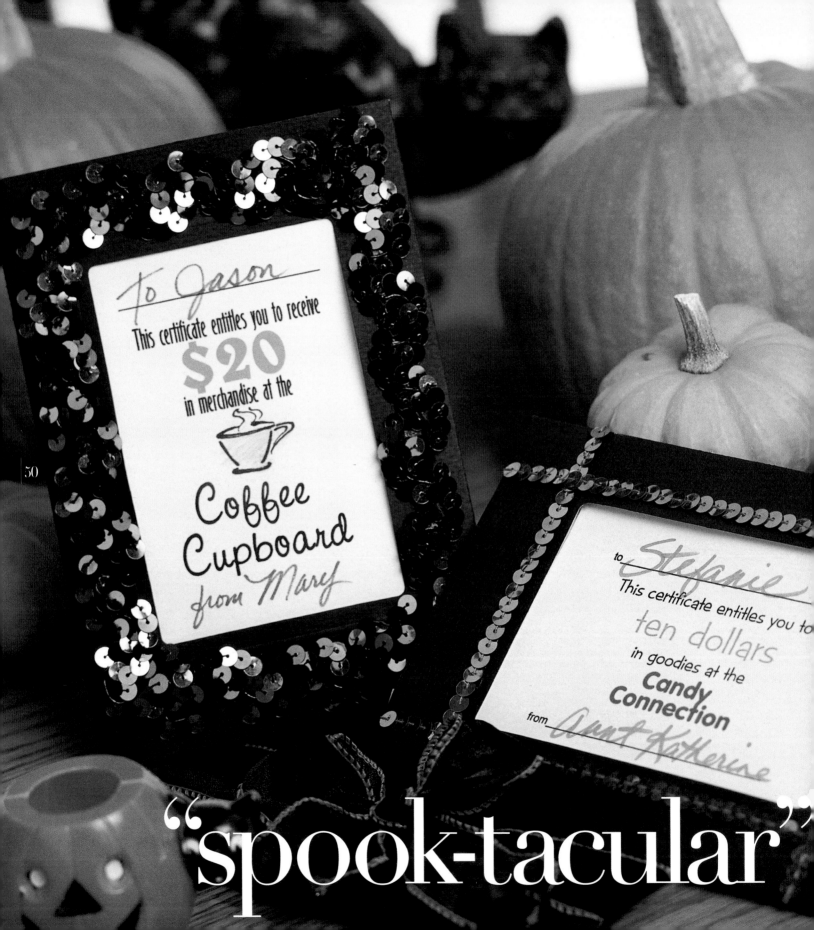

To Jason

This certificate entitles you to receive

$20

in merchandise at the

Coffee Cupboard

from Mary

to *Stefanie*

This certificate entitles you to

ten dollars

in goodies at the

Candy Connection

from *Aunt Katherine*

"spook-tacular"

sparkling sequin frame

make it in minutes

to make the
frame you'll
need:
Black die-cut
   photo cards with
   envelopes
Sequin trim in
   orange and black
Scissors
Thick white crafts
   glue
Gift certificate
Tape
Black and orange
   ribbon

here's how

To make this project, cut sections of sequin trim to fit around card front and on the envelope flap. Glue the sequins in place. Let the glue dry. Place a gift certificate in the opening of the card. From the back side, tape the gift certificate in place. Place the card in the envelope and tie with a ribbon bow.

Hand-draw or computer-generate your own personalized gift certificates for:

- Car washes
- Back rubs
- Cleaning
- Dinner and a movie
- A night on the town
- Baby-sitting
- Breakfast in bed
- A day at the zoo
- Washing dishes

51

This surprise will haunt them in a good way—
a sequined frame for a gift certificate.

1 more idea...
Decorate a photo mat using this technique
to frame a trick-or-treat photograph.

also try this...
Place an invitation in the cutout for an
extra-special party invite.

Happy Halloween

"eerie-sistible'

fiendish flowers

make it in minutes

to make the
flower vase
you'll need:
12-inch length of
¼-inch square
dowel
Acrylic paints in
white and black
¼-inch flat
paintbrush
Heavy paper in
black and white
Pinking shears
and/or other
decorative-edge
scissors
Glue stick
Black marking pen
Strong clear
adhesive, such
as E6000
16-inch-long piece
of ½-inch-wide
ribbon
Rose bowl
with flair
at rim
Approximately
16 Halloween
erasers
Fresh flowers

here's how

To make this project, paint the dowel white. Let the paint dry. Paint black stripes on all sides of dowel, allowing ¼ inch of white to show between stripes. Let dry.

Cut a 2x3-inch piece of black paper using decorative-edge scissors. Cut a slightly smaller piece from white. Use a glue stick to adhere the white paper onto the center of the black paper. Write a Halloween message on the tag. Use strong adhesive to glue the tag at an angle on one end of the dowel.

Tie a ribbon around the neck of the rose bowl. Using strong adhesive, glue erasers on the tag, in the center of the bow, and randomly on the rose bowl. Let the adhesive dry. Fill the vase halfway with water and add a small floral bouquet.

A mini bouquet in Halloween colors will surely lift anyone's spirit.

1 more idea...
Pin a Halloween brooch onto center of the bow.

also try this...
Fill the vase with silk flowers for an everlasting bouquet.

sequin-studded plate

make it in minutes

Transform an ordinary paper plate into a "boo-tiful" serving piece more quickly than a witch can cast a spell.

54

here's how

To make this plate, measure and mark ¾-inch intervals around the plate. Use a paper punch to make a hole by each mark, ¼ inch from the plate edge. Place an eyelet in the hole of a sequin and then into a hole in the plate. Use the eyelet tool to secure sequin in place. Continue working in this manner by overlapping the sequins and alternating the sequin and eyelet colors.

1 more idea...
Add a sequin border to plastic place mats for a coordinating Halloween touch.

also try this...
Punch holes in large confetti; then add the different shapes to the border.

55

entertaining

thankful

gilded cornucopia

make it in minutes

This everlasting seasonal treasure is the perfect gift
to present to your Thanksgiving host or hostess.

to make the
cornucopia
you'll need:
Small wicker
   cornucopia
Hot-glue gun
Hot-glue sticks
Braided trim
Upholstery tack
Newspapers
Floral tape and wire
Wire cutters
Assorted silk fruits
   and leaves
Newspapers
White spray primer
Gold spray paint
Yellow glass spray
   paint or yellow
   transparent spray
   paint
Red glitter spray
Foam ball, such as
   Styrofoam,
   to fit into
   cornucopia

here's how

To make this project, wind braided trim around the cornucopia, starting with the tip of the cornucopia. Secure with hot glue and one upholstery tack. Continue gluing the braid around the cornucopia until covered.

Attach a piece of wire to fruit and leaves. Use floral tape to secure if necessary. In a well-ventilated work area, cover work surface with newspaper. Spray fruit and leaves with primer. Let dry. Spray with gold paint. Let dry. Spray a light coat of yellow glass paint over the gold. Let dry. Highlight the tops of fruit and leaves with light sprays of red glitter. Let dry.

Insert foam ball into the cornucopia. Arrange wired leaves toward the sides of the cornucopia, inserting the wires into the foam ball. Arrange the fruit in the middle.

1 more idea...
Use a basket in place of a cornucopia to display the gilded fruit.

also try this...
Gild and glitter artificial fruit to insert into a grapevine wreath.

glamorous gourds
make it in minutes

Straight pins
Trim, such as
   rickrack and
   beaded string
Scissors
Real or artificial
   gourds

to make the
wrap you'll
need:
Glass plate
White gift box
Shredded paper
Rickrack in
   assorted sizes
Hot-glue gun and
   glue sticks

58

here's how

To make this project, pin the end of the desired trim next to the gourd stem. Bring the trim to the bottom of the gourd or wrap around the gourd. Pin the trim in place. Cut off the excess trim. Continue decorating the gourd in this manner until you achieve the look you want. Cut off any excess trim and secure the ends with pins.

presentation

For coordinating wrap, place the gourds on a plate and place in a white gift box. Cushion contents with shredded paper. Glue rickrack around the box, laying the rickrack in both directions. Add a ribbon bow and a gift tag.

Add an elegant flair to small white gourds using snippets of rickrack and beaded string.

1 more idea...
Use large rickrack, beads, ribbon,
and braid to decorate pumpkins.

also try this...
Decorate artificial pears and other fruit
with trims for an unexpected touch.

naturally
elegant

good ideas candied flowerpots

Hard candies transform ordinary terra-cotta pots
into cheerful holiday servers. Simply hot-glue the
candies around the rim of a painted pot and let cool.
Fill the pot with sweets of the season. Or place a
votive candle in a painted terra-cotta pot saucer for
a last-minute holiday gift.

snowflake coasters
make it in minutes

to make the coasters you'll need:
Scissors
Ruler
Felt in two contrasting colors
White mesh tulle
½ yard of ⅜-inch-wide velvet ribbon to match base-color felt for each coaster
Various sequins, including snowflake shapes
Fabric glue

62

to make the gift wrap you'll need:
Box to fit coasters
Purple wrapping paper
Tape
Pencil
Thick white crafts glue
Small white buttons
Curling ribbon

here's how

To make this project, cut a 4¼-inch square from the base-color felt and from the mesh tulle. Cut four 4¼-inch lengths of velvet ribbon. Enlarge a snowflake sequin on a photocopier until it is 3 inches in diameter. Use this as a pattern to cut a snowflake out of the contrasting felt. Glue the felt snowflake to the center of the felt square. Sprinkle a few sequins over the felt snowflake, keeping them toward the center of the square. Lay the square of mesh tulle on top of the felt square and snowflake; line up the edges. Put a bead of fabric glue ⅛ inch from the edge of the coaster on all four sides. Dab additional glue on the back of each piece of ribbon. Lay the four pieces of velvet ribbon along the edges of the coaster and press them into the glue, overlapping corners. Let dry.

presentation

For a coordinating wrap, place the coasters in a box and wrap with purple wrapping paper. Draw three intersecting lines forming a snowflake shape. Glue buttons over the lines. Let dry. Add curling ribbon and a gift tag if desired.

A set of these no-sew sparkly, soft snowflake coasters is a thoughtful gift for a holiday party host.

1 more idea...
Make snowflake place mats, sewing or gluing the sequins in place.

also try this...
Use holiday confetti to add interest to the coasters.

wintry

très lovely

ribbon tray

make it in minutes

to make the
tray you'll need:
Newspapers
Small metal tray
 with rim
White spray primer
Red spray paint
Assorted ribbons
Scissors
Decoupage
 medium
Paintbrush

To make a lasting impression,
accompany a food gift with
a stunning ribbon tray.

here's how

To make this project, use newspapers to cover the work surface in a well-ventilated work area. Spray the top of the tray with primer. Let dry. Spray the rim area red. Let dry. Apply a second coat if necessary. Let dry. Cut pieces of ribbon to fit the center of the tray. Working in small strips, paint decoupage medium onto the tray. Lay a ribbon in place and press firmly. Continue working in this manner until the center of the tray is filled with ribbons. Apply decoupage medium over the top of the ribbons. Let dry.

65

1 more idea...
Decoupage ribbons on a wood
charger and use with clear glass plates.

also try this...
Decoupage ribbons onto a mirror
or picture frame.

salad mold trims
make it in minutes

to make the ornaments you'll need:
Drill and large bit
Small salad molds
Newspapers
Spray paint in
    desired colors
Glitter in color
    similar to
    spray paint
Jewelry
    embellishments
    or ornate buttons
Strong adhesive,
    such as E6000
Scissors
Ribbon

here's how
To make this project, drill a hole at the top of each mold. Place the salad mold on newspapers in a well-ventilated work area. Spray the top side of mold with spray paint. While paint is wet, sprinkle with glitter. Let dry. Turn over the mold and spray again. Let dry. Glue jewelry piece or button in the center of the rounded portion of the mold. Let dry. Thread a ribbon through the hole for hanging and knot the ribbon ends. Trim the ribbon ends if needed.

66

Vintage or new, small salad molds decorated as trims
make wonderful last-minute gifts.

1 more idea...
Glue two of the same shape molds back to
back for a two-sided ornament.

also try this...
Use a white permanent marker to add
handwritten sentiments on flat surfaces
of the molds.

ornamental

surprise

jingle bell bag

make it in minutes

to make the
bag you'll need:
Scissors
Pearls on a string
Purchased red
  velour marble bag
Green metallic
  thread
Sewing needle
Small jingle bells in
  green and silver
Three snowflake
  sequins

Tiny treasures await in this velour bag
that glistens with silver and green.

here's how

To make this project, cut a length of pearls to fit around
the top of the bag. Stitch in place with metallic green thread,
tacking between each pearl. Sew jingle bells on the bottom of
the bag, alternating green and silver. Sew on three snowflake
sequins vertically, adding a tiny green jingle bell in each center.
Sew three silver jingle bells on the end of the drawstring.

69

1 more idea...
Use holiday buttons or
charms in place of the
snowflake sequins.

also try this...
Decorate a tote bag for the holidays
using the same festive embellishments.

embroidered throw

make it in minutes

70

to make the throw you'll need:

Purchased 50×66-inch plaid wool throw with fringed ends
7×50-inch piece of fusible interfacing
Assorted velvet, grosgrain, and tapestry ribbons ranging from ⅜ to 1 inch wide
Thread
3-ply wool yarn
#3 and #5 pearl cotton

Keep a loved one cuddly warm with a soft wool throw adorned with colorful embroidery stitches.

here's how

To make this project, place the interfacing on the wrong side of the throw, approximately 3 inches from the fringe. Topstitch ribbons on the right side over interfacing, allowing space between ribbons. Turn the short ends of the ribbons to the back of the throw and stitch to secure. Referring to the stitch diagrams, *right,* work embroidery stitches over the ribbons using desired colors of wool yarn or pearl cotton.

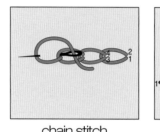

chain stitch

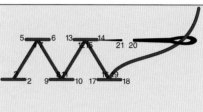

chevron stitch

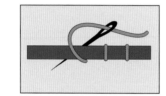

couching

cross stitch

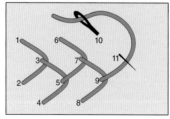

feather stitch

french knot

lazy daisy

1 more idea...
Spruce up a flannel shirt by adding embroidered ribbons to the pockets.

also try this...
Add dimension to the ribbon design by incorporating buttons and beads.

warmth

good ideas candied candlelight

Canning jars display a playful glow when holding a white taper candle nestled in holiday candy. For a delightful presentation, place a clear cellophane bag in the jar. Fill the bag halfway with wrapped or unwrapped candies and secure with a twist tie. Use raffia to tie a candle to the outside of the jar.

sweet caroling cherubs
make it in minutes

to make a cherub you'll need:
1-inch wood ball with drilled hole
10-inch-long dowel to fit into ball
Thick white crafts glue
Acrylic paints in golden brown, peach, brown, and gold
Small flat or round paintbrush
Small stencil brush
Very fine liner brush
Clear sealer
Yarn
10-inch-long piece of 2-inch-wide gold wired ribbon
Thread
Hot-glue gun and glue sticks
Satin flower
⅛-inch-wide ribbon

Singing the joys of the season, these heavenly angels are wonderful gifts for teachers, friends, and neighbors.

here's how

To make this project, insert the dowel into the wood ball. Glue into place and let dry. Paint the wood ball with the desired flesh color. Let dry. Paint a round gold cap on the head. Let dry. To paint cheeks, use the stencil brush and very little peach paint. Using a fine liner brush, paint the eyes brown. For each eye, paint a half-moon shape with eyelashes. Paint a small brown oval for the mouth. Let dry. Paint wood head with sealer.

Run a line of glue along the edge of the dowel. Pull one end out from a skein of yarn and fasten tightly below the head. Wind yarn around the entire dowel, keeping the wraps smooth and even. Continue winding around the dowel to make the body shape wide at the top and narrow at the bottom.

To make wings, fold the ends of the gold wired ribbon in toward the center, overlapping at least 1 inch in the middle. With thread, wind and tie very tightly around the center of ribbon to hold it together and make a bow shape.

Hot-glue it to the back of the angel right below the head. Apply hot glue to the flower and place it on the front of the angel right below the chin. Make a small ribbon loop and hot-glue it to the back for hanging.

1 more idea...
Personalize cherubs by replacing the flower with a meaningful charm.

also try this...
Paint a variety of facial expressions to give each angel personality.

angelic

charming

vintage stockings
make it in minutes

stocking pattern
(1 square = 1 inch)

here's how

To make this project, enlarge and trace the pattern, *above,* and cut out. Use the pattern to cut two stocking shapes from the tea towel. Cut a 1x5-inch piece of fabric for a hanging loop. Cut two corners from napkin or tea towel, each equal to the width of the stocking top and approximately one-half the stocking height.

Stitch the stocking pieces with the right sides together using ½-inch seams. Leave the top open. Clip and trim the seam. Turn the stocking to the right side.

For the hanging loop, press in ¼ inch along two long edges. Press in half lengthwise and topstitch. Fold the loop in half crosswise and baste the raw edge at the back seam.

Seam the cuff in a continuous loop. Stitch lace along the bottom edge of cuff. Weave ribbon through the lace if desired and tie ends into a bow. Match the side seams on the right side of the cuff to the wrong side of stocking. Stitch around the top edge. Fold the cuff to the right side.

to make a
stocking you'll
need:
Tracing paper
Pencil
Scissors
18x28-inch vintage
   or new tea towel
   for stocking
Vintage or new
   fabric napkin or
   tea towel for cuff
Lace
Needle
Thread
⅛- or ¼-inch-wide
   ribbon

77

Vintage linens find their place during the holidays as reinvented Christmas stockings to give with love.

● *1 more idea...*
Give new linens vintage appeal by dyeing in a strong tea solution.

● *also try this...*
If you don't have a fireplace, hang the stockings on a railing or along a windowsill.

temptation

etched cookie jar

step-by-step

This ornamental jar is perfect for giving all the season's sweet surprises.

to make the cookie jar you'll need:
Glass jar with lid
Newspapers
Tracing or typing
  paper
Scissors
Pencil with
  round-tip eraser
Tape
Etching cream
Small round,
  fine-tip, and
  ½-inch flat
  paintbrushes
Rubber gloves
Disposable foam
  plate
Acrylic glass
  paints in red,
  white, green,
  teal, purple,
  and silver
Red
  metallic
  cord
3 medium
  jingle bells

cookie jar etching and painting pattern

The instructions are on pages 80–81.

● *1 more idea...*
For a year-round design,
etch a family name and embellish
it with painted flowers.

● *also try this...*
Tape simple holiday greeting cards on
the inside of the jar to use as patterns.

etched cookie jar (continued)

1 **Wash the jar and let it dry.** Avoid touching the areas to be painted.

2 **Cover the work surface** with newspapers. Trace the pattern, *page 79,* onto tracing or typing paper. If necessary, reduce or enlarge the pattern on a copy machine to fit your jar. Trim any extra paper away from the design. Tape the pattern to the inside of the jar.

3 **Using etching cream,** paint the words on the outside of the jar as shown by the pattern. Be very careful as the glass will etch wherever the cream is applied. Read the directions on the etching cream label to know how long to let the cream stay on the glass.

4 **Put on rubber gloves.** When time is up for the etching cream, rinse off the cream under the faucet. Dry the jar.

5 **Place some red paint** on a foam plate. Using a fine-tip brush, add a shadow to the left side of the letters as shown, *left*. Let the paint dry.

6 **Add white highlights** to the top of each letter. Let the paint dry.

7 **Place green, teal, and white paints** on the disposable plate. Drag the flat brush through each color, and begin to add sprigs of greenery around the lettering and on the jar lid. Start from the center of the sprig and brush outward. Continue making these strokes until you reach the desired length. Let the paint dry.

8 **Add berries by dipping** the eraser end of a pencil into red paint and dotting it on the surface. To add garlands, follow this same method with desired colors of paint mixed with white. Let the paint dry.

9 **String three jingle bells** onto the cord. Tie around the lid knob.

good ideas boots for barkers

What dog wouldn't appreciate these paw-warming booties filled with a good-dog assortment of treats? Choose long treats to place in each boot, adding other items such as a leash or small toy to make the gift complete.

decorate

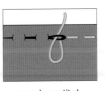

old-fashioned trims

make it in minutes

**to make
either ornament
you'll need:**
Tracing or typing
    paper
Pencil
Scissors
Pins
Felt in desired
    colors
Fabric glue
Embroidery floss in
    a color to contrast
    felt colors
Needle
Assorted holiday
    buttons and
    charms, including
    a star button
8-inch-long piece
    of ¼-inch ribbon
Fiberfill

here's how

**To make an
ornament,** enlarge
and trace the desired
pattern, *left or below,*
onto tracing or typing
paper. Cut out the
pattern pieces. Pin the
patterns to the desired
colors of felt. Cut out
the irregular felt
shapes. Cut two of
the background.

Arrange the irregular pieces on top of one
background piece with no space between pieces.
Glue the pieces in place.

Using three plies of embroidery floss, stitch over the
seams using a herringbone stitch (diagram *below*) as
shown, *above* and *right*. Stitch around edges with a
running stitch. Use floss that contrasts with felt color.

Sew on all buttons (except star button) and charms
referring to the photograph, *opposite,* for placement.

Pin the ornament front on top of the remaining
background piece. Fold ribbon piece in half. Put the
ends between the two background pieces. Center

the ribbon for the tree or put in the right corner for
the stocking.

Stitch the edges of the background pieces
together using blanket stitches, stopping 2 inches
from the beginning stitch. Stuff the ornament with
fiberfill, then continue with the blanket stitch.

Sew a star button to the top of the tree or the
top right corner of the stocking.

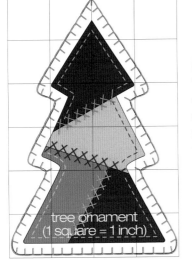

tree ornament
(1 square = 1 inch)

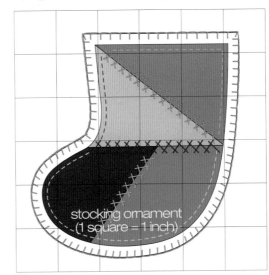

stocking ornament
(1 square = 1 inch)

85

Pieced felt joined by delicate stitches lends a
country feel to these keepsake ornaments.

● *1 more idea...*
Use cookie cutters to make
other simple holiday shapes.

● *also try this...*
Use patterns to make paper
tags to adorn gifts.

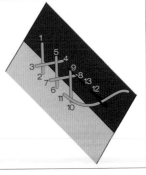

herringbone stitch

blanket stitch

running stitch

good ideas ribbon candy holders

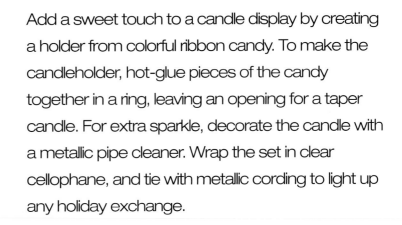

Add a sweet touch to a candle display by creating a holder from colorful ribbon candy. To make the candleholder, hot-glue pieces of the candy together in a ring, leaving an opening for a taper candle. For extra sparkle, decorate the candle with a metallic pipe cleaner. Wrap the set in clear cellophane, and tie with metallic cording to light up any holiday exchange.

greetings

Heartiest greetings for Christmas and sincere good wishes for the New Year.

postcard pillow

make it in minutes

here's how

To make this pillow, center the enlarged postcard design on an 11x7-inch piece of photo transfer paper at a photocopy center, creating a mirror image of the design. Transfer the design onto the white fabric according to the manufacturer's directions.

Cut two wool horizontal sashing strips and two vertical sashing strips, each 2½x11 inches. Cut a 16½x12½-inch wool back. For taffeta ruffle, cut 4½-inch-wide bias strips that are twice the perimeter of the pillow, piecing the fabric as necessary.

Using ¼-inch seams, stitch horizontal sashing strips to the top and bottom edge of the white fabric with the transferred design. Stitch the vertical sashing strips to each side of the design.

For ruffle, stitch the taffeta bias strip ends together to form a continuous loop. Press ruffle fabric in half, wrong sides facing. Gather raw edges. Stitch ruffle around the outside edge of the pillow front.

With right sides facing, stitch pillow front to back around outside edge, keeping ruffle free and leaving an opening for turning. Trim the corners. Turn to right side. Insert the pillow form and stitch the opening closed. Hand-stitch lace on around the design in the center of the sashing strips.

Share a favorite classic postcard by transferring the greeting to pillow-making fabric.

1 more idea...

Use a family photograph to display on a year-round pillow.

also try this...

Sew large or clusters of small jingle bells to the corners of the pillow.

heartfelt

be mine bath beads

make it in minutes

Send a pampering gift to someone dear to your heart with this thoughtful bath collection.

to make the
bath package
you'll need:
Bath items to wrap,
  such as
  purchased bath
  salts in clear
  plastic bag, soap,
  or bath beads
Sheer pink fabric
Waxed paper
White fabric paint
Scissors
Sheer white ribbon

here's how

To make this project, lay the bath items on fabric to determine how large a piece of fabric is needed. Lay fabric on waxed paper. Draw a wavy outline around edge to be trimmed. Draw hearts, lines, squiggles, or other designs onto pink fabric. Let dry.
Cut out fabric, right along edge of white fabric paint. Lay items on fabric and roll up; or bring edges up and tie with sheer ribbon.

91

1 more idea...
Instead of ribbon, secure the fabric with pearls strung on a fine wire.

also try this...
Add a cassette or compact disc of soothing music to this pampering gift.

treasured

metallic hearts

make it in minutes

to make a necklace you will need:
Instant papier-mâché, such as Celluclay
Plastic bag
Tongue depressor or crafts stick
Small screw eye, jump ring, and cording
Thick white crafts glue
Black acrylic paint
Paintbrush
Desired color of metallic leaf, adhesive, and sealer
Soft cloth
Small beads, brass hearts, sequins, or other embellishments
Sequin pins

here's how

To make this project, mix papier-mâché according to the directions, approximately 1 cup papier-mâché to ¼ cup water, in a plastic bag. Knead it until it becomes as smooth as bread dough. This quantity will make enough dough for four or five hearts.

Pinch off two pieces of dough. Roll each one into a ball and then narrow one end into a cone shape. Join the two together with the narrow ends at the bottom. Smooth the edges together with fingers or a tongue depressor. If needed, dampen fingers with water, and smooth out the surface of the heart. If making a necklace, insert screw eye before drying. Let dry.

Use glue to hold a loosened screw eye or the two sections together if they separate during drying. Let glue dry.

Paint both sides of heart with black paint and set aside to dry. Apply adhesive to heart. When tacky, place small pieces of metallic leaf on heart and burnish (rub firmly) with a soft cloth. Apply a coat of sealer.

Use sequin pins to pin beads, sequins, and brass charms to hearts. Add jump ring to screw eye. Thread cord through the jump ring.

Ask someone to be your valentine with these papier-mâché hearts drenched in gold and silver.

1 more idea...

Make flatter versions of these hearts to mount on natural paper and frame.

also try this...

Use screw eyes to link several hearts together. Hang on a front door or from the center of a chandelier.

be mine

paper valentines

make it in minutes

Made from playful scrapbooking papers,
these heart-to-heart cards will spread affection
to beloved friends and family.

here's how

To make a valentine, trace the desired template with a light pencil line on the wrong side of desired paper. Using regular scissors or decorative-edge scissors, cut out shape.

For bookmarks, postcards, and tags, use decorative-edge scissors to trim the edges if desired.

Decide on the paper punch design and placement. Punch holes first to make it easier to place the stickers and draw in decorative lines.

To apply stickers, peel off the back of each sticker and place on cutout,

angling and overlapping as desired. Embellish stickers by outlining with color-coordinated metallic or sparkle gel pens.

Fill in blank areas with additional line drawings, using the patterns on *page 96* if desired. Use one of the paper punches to add punched holes, and/or crafts glue to add buttons.

Weave ribbon through larger punched holes, either just at the top, to one side, or circling a design. Tie the ends in a bow and trim. Add a matching ribbon hanger if desired.

Instructions continue on page 96.

1 more idea...
Use these valentine ideas for laying out pages in a scrapbook.

also try this...
Use the patterns on the following two pages for decorating plain stationery and envelopes with marking pens.

to make a
Valentine you'll
need:
Purchased templates in the shapes of hearts, ovals, and rectangles
8½x11-inch pieces of card stock in pure white, soft white, shades of red, and lavender
Patterned scrapbook papers
Vellum in frosted white with swirls and frosted white with red hearts
Precut white scalloped postcards
Decorative-edge scissors
Precut white bookmarks
Precut white tags
Paper punches in desired shapes
Metallic gel pens in white, lavender, red, pink, blush, silver, and gold
Sparkle gel pens in red, pink, and blush
A variety of valentine stickers
Alphabet stickers in white and red
Buttons in white and shades of pink
Thick white crafts glue
Paper crimper
Assorted ribbons
Spacers, such as Pop Dots, in ⅛- and ¹⁄₁₆-inch thicknesses
Scissors

paper valentines (continued)

For the scalloped heart cutouts with vellum overlay, use a template to trace on the wrong side of card stock or patterned paper. Cut out shape. Repeat on the vellum paper and cut just inside of the traced line. Lay vellum heart on top of the card stock heart and carefully embellish with desired paper punch. Loop a ribbon hanger through punches on top center and tie a bow.

For the crimped designs, roll design through the crimper after punching holes, applying stickers, and drawing decorative lines. Add desired buttons and/or ribbon after crimping.

For 3-D designs, apply stickers of choice to small pieces of coordinating colors of card stock. Trim close all around the edges of the sticker with straight or decorative-edge scissors. Apply the spacers, following the package instructions. Attach spacers to card as desired.

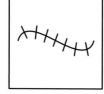
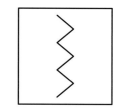

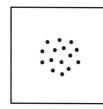

hugs and kisses

fancy floral frame

make it in minutes

to make the
frame you'll
need:

Newspapers
Wide picture frame
with white inset or
mat
Bright pink spray
paint
Alphabet macaroni,
acini di pepe, shell
and elbow
macaroni, and
ditalini
Acrylic enamel
paints in bright
pink, red, pink,
purple, green,
white, and yellow
Paintbrush
Strong adhesive,
such as E6000

99

here's how

To make the frame, in a well-ventilated work area, cover the work surface with newspapers. Spray-paint the frame. Let dry.

Glue alphabet macaroni on the inset to spell "Be Mine," placing an X and O between phrases. Let dry. Paint the letters bright pink. Paint the Xs and Os red. Let dry.

To make a petaled flower, glue five shells in a circle. Glue ditalini in the center. Add shell leaves. Let dry. To make a rose, hook together two pieces of elbow macaroni. Add three thin elbows to complete the circle. Add an elbow stem and shell leaves. Glue in place. Let dry.

Glue pieces of acini di pepe between the flowers. Let dry. Paint the petaled flowers pink and the centers purple. Paint the roses red. Paint the leaves and stems green. Paint the dots white. Let dry. Paint white highlights on pink petals. Paint pink on the purple flower centers and on the roses. Paint yellow on the petals and stems. Let dry.

Whether you want to show off a photo, drawing, or poem, this floral frame makes a heartfelt gift.

● *1 more idea...*
Select a phrase from a poem to spell out on the inset.

● *also try this...*
Use white seed beads in place of acini di pepe.

good ideas from-the-heart bouquet

Send a gift of flowers that will never be forgotten.
Place a Valentine's Day bouquet in a creamy white
pitcher tied with a bright red bow. For the heart tags,
use the pattern below to trace and cut two tags
from red paper. Outline each heart with glue and
sprinkle with red glitter. Write a message on each
heart using a white paint pen.

heart pattern

whimsical

jelly bean candles

step-by-step

A favorite Easter candy adds a playful touch to molded candles.

to make a
candle you'll
need:
Clear candle wax
Old pan and can
Metal gelatin molds
Awl
Custard cup
Small white birthday
   candles
Small jelly beans in
   assorted colors

1 **Break the wax** into small pieces. Place wax in the can. Place the can in the pan. Fill the pan halfway with water. Place the pan on the stove and turn on the stove. Heat the wax only until it is just melted, then reduce the heat. Never use a microwave to melt wax.

2 **Using an awl,** make a small hole in top of mold. Invert mold into custard cup to keep it level. Place a birthday candle upside down into the hole of the mold. This will be the candle wick.

3 **Place a few jelly beans** in the bottom of the mold. Pour a little wax into the mold. Keep adding the jelly beans and the wax until the mold is full. Allow the wax to cool completely. Invert the mold to release the candle.

■ Note: Do not light candles close to Easter grass. Never leave burning candles unattended.

103

1 more idea...
Look for gummies in Easter shapes to adorn these mini candles.

also try this...
Nest the candles in a short cut-glass dish filled with jelly beans.

pastel pails
make it in minutes

to make the
pails you'll
need:

Aluminum
   containers
Newspapers
Transparent spray
   paints in desired
   colors, such as
   Boyd model car
   paint (available in
   hobby shops)
Glitter tube-style
   paint
Sequin trims
Hot-glue gun
Hot-glue sticks

here's how

To make this project, wash and dry the container.
In a well-ventilated work area, cover work surface with
newspapers. Spray the pail with two or three light coats of
paint, allowing the paint to dry between coats. Using glitter
paint, draw simple random patterns, such as lines, shapes,
and circles. Let dry. Use hot glue to affix sequin trim around
the top edge. Let dry.

104

Here's a simple gift that even Peter
Cottontail would love to give.

1 more idea...
Use this technique on metal watering
cans, tin cans, and sap buckets.

also try this...
After Easter, use the pail as a flowerpot
for indoor plants.

dazzling

pride

106

for-mom flowerpot

make it in minutes

When the kids are longing to make
you something for Mother's Day, lend a hand in
creating this smile-raising flowerpot.

107

here's how

To make a flowerpot, cover the work surface in a well-ventilated work area with newspapers. Spray two light coats of white spray primer onto the outside of a clean, dry pot. Let dry.

Sponge a generous amount of white acrylic paint onto surface. Sponge a small amount of pale green and gold onto white. Let dry. Hot-glue braid around rim. Tie a ribbon bow below braid.

On photo, draw a circle around the face using a pencil. If you wish to preserve the photo, make a photocopy and draw the circle on the copy. Using a glue stick, attach the photo to card stock. Cut out circle shape with scissors. Cut a second circle out of card stock for the back side. Hot-glue fringe to the back of photo. Hot-glue a gold pipe-cleaner stem onto the back side of photo.

Hot-glue the braid to the back of the photo circle on both sides, clipping braid as necessary to help curve around circle.

Fill pot with soil. Position bulbs according to instructions for depth. Cover top of soil with green moss. Insert picture flower and several curved stems of pipe cleaners.

1 more idea...
For a teacher who is really sweet, fill the flowerpot with wrapped candies instead of potting soil.

also try this...
Decorate the pot with the child's handprints, by placing hand in acrylic paint, then pressing on the surface of the pot.

keepsake

place mat scrapbook

make it in minutes

to make the
book you'll
need:
Plastic place mats
Scissors
Photo sheets,
   index cards, or
   card stock sheets
Ribbon
Butterflies and/or
   silk flower
   sections
Paper punch
Crafts wire
Thick white
   crafts glue

This Mother's Day, give her something she'll love to boast about—a flowery scrapbook to show off photos and other important memorabilia.

here's how

To make the scrapbook front and back covers, cut two sections of place mat ½ to 1 inch wider and taller than the photo sheets, index cards, or card stock. If using cards or paper, punch two to three holes along the left edge of each sheet. Punch corresponding holes in the cut covers. Stack the sheets inside the covers and then tie a ribbon section through each hole. Wire or glue butterflies or flowers to one of the ribbons.

1 more idea...

Laminate a collage of photocopied ticket stubs, map pieces, letters, or other keepsakes for an interesting scrapbook cover.

also try this...

Cut plastic place mats to make dividers in school notebooks.

jeweled paperweights
make it in minutes

to make a paperweight you'll need:
New or vintage transparent paperweights with removable backs
Pencil
Tracing paper
Scissors
White felt
Cardboard
Decorative buttons, brooches, or pendants
Strong adhesive, such as E6000

110

here's how
To make a paperweight, trace around the bottom to make a pattern. Cut out. Trace around the pattern on felt twice and on cardboard once. Cut out shapes. Glue a piece of felt to each side of the cardboard cutout. Let dry. Glue the decorative piece in the center on one side of the felt disk. Let dry. Glue the paperweight atop the embellished felt piece. Let dry.

Whether you want to preserve a piece of family history or simply capture a pretty shape under glass, making a paperweight as a gift is a wonderful way to protect and pass on something special.

1 more idea...
Glue the item atop a handwritten poem or letter for a personal touch.

also try this...
Use a gold metallic marking pen to add designs around the edge of the paperweight.

heirloom

enlighten

father's day lamp

step-by-step

to make the
spring lamp
you'll need:
Lamp kit with metal
  base
Lamp rod
Spring long enough
  to cover lamp rod
Large nut, washer,
  and small nut
Desired lampshade

to make the
hardware lamp
you'll need:
Lamp kit with
  black base
Assorted metal,
  plastic, and
  rubber nuts and
  washers to fit
  over the lamp rod
Black lampshade

to make the
bamboo lamp
you'll need:
Lamp kit with
  natural wood
  base
Bamboo
Utility knife
Raffia
Polished stones
Hot-glue gun
Hot-glue sticks
Artificial dragonfly
Desired lampshade

Hunt the jungle, comb the beach, or search the hardware store to discover the materials for these handsome reading lamps for Dad.

Instructions are on pages 114–115.

1 more idea...
Cover the lamp rod with rolled up newspapers for Dad's office.

also try this...
Drill through the center of toy cars for a childhood spin on this project.

father's day lamp (continued)

SPRING LAMP

1 Slide the spring over the lamp rod. Secure at the top with a large nut, a washer, and a small nut.

2 Assemble the lamp top and add the shade.

HARDWARE LAMP

1 Place washers, nuts, and bolts over the lamp rod randomly or in a repeated pattern.

2 Assemble the lamp top and add the shade.

BAMBOO LAMP

1 **Cut approximately 15 lengths** of bamboo ¾ inch shorter than lamp rod. Arrange bamboo pieces around the lamp rod. Place a rubber band around the bundle to hold in place. Cut three 2-foot lengths of raffia. Tie the raffia around the bamboo in three areas to secure. Remove the rubber band.

2 **Arrange polished stones** on lamp base. Hot-glue stones in place.

115

3 **Assemble the lamp top** and add the shade. Hot-glue an artificial dragonfly to the lampshade, allowing one wing to drape off edge of shade.

good ideas for father

Tell your dad he's the best there is with either of these nostalgic gift ideas. For a book lover, place a family photograph on a stack of vintage books and tie with a pair of generous ribbon bows. To surprise a golf enthusiast, fill a black pail with an interesting mix of new and collectible golf memorabilia. Add a black and white gingham bow to complete the presentation.

sparkling starfish
make it in minutes

to make the
starfish you'll
need:

Newspapers
3 starfish
Spray paints in red,
   white, and blue
Glitter in red, white,
   and blue
Red towels
Red, white, and
   blue ribbon

A perfect gift for the Fourth of July,
                    these stars will sparkle all year long.

present*ation*

118

here's how

To make the starfish, cover the
work surface with newspapers in a
well-ventilated work area. Spray-paint
the starfish one at a time with the
desired color of spray paint. Let dry.
Add a second coat and, while the
paint is wet, sprinkle with the same
color of glitter. Let dry. Repeat for the
remaining starfish. Group one red,
one white, and one blue starfish for a
patriotic effect. Tie the three starfish
to a set of red towels.

For a coordinating wrap, place the starfish in a box lined
with shredded paper. Wrap the box with blue paper. Use red
glitter tube-style paint to draw random horizontal lines on the
package. Use silver glitter tube-style paint to add accents. Let
dry. Cut a star shape from a ½-inch-thick sponge. Paint with
several layers of silver glitter paint. Let dry. Glue sponge on
package top.

1 more idea...
Make enough glittered starfish
to make a patriotic garland for the
front porch or banister.

also try this...
Use bright metallic spray paints for
someone with contemporary tastes.

patriotic

celebration jewelry
make it in minutes

to make the
jewelry you'll
need:
Scissors
Elastic thread
Drill and small bit
Dice in red, white,
    and blue
Silver beads

here's how

To make a bracelet, cut a 10-inch length of elastic. Drill through the centers of approximately nine dice. Thread dice and beads onto the elastic, alternating as you work. Fit on wrist occasionally for size. Knot ends of elastic together. Trim excess elastic.

To make a necklace, cut a 30-inch length of elastic. Thread on 8 inches of silver beads. Drill through the centers of three dice, one of each color. Thread on the red die, a bead, the white die, a bead, the blue die, and 8 more inches of silver beads. Try on the necklace to determine the length. Add more silver beads on each end of the elastic if desired. Knot the ends together. Trim excess elastic.

120

Dice and silver beads make an
        interesting combination in this
        fun-and-games approach to red, white,
and blue jewelry—a perfect gift for
        Independence Day or any day!

1 more idea...
Replace seven of the bracelet beads with
alphabet beads that spell *America*.

also try this...
Make small bracelets to use as
Fourth of July napkin rings.

playful

play ball

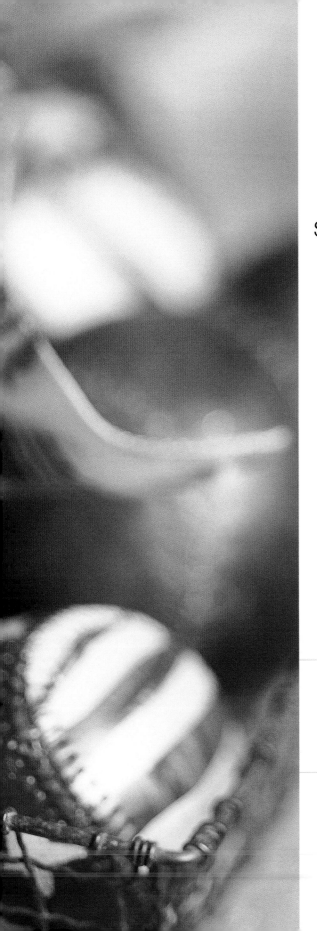

patriotic play
make it in minutes

Symbols of a favorite American
sport, these baseballs tout the
red, white, and blue — and make
a perfect hostess gift for
a backyard picnic.

to make the
baseballs
you'll need:
New or used
   baseballs and
   softballs
Acrylic paints in red,
   navy, and cream
Stencil brushes
Small paintbrushes
Star stencil
Paste wax

here's how
To make a baseball, paint the ball using the
seams as guides to separate colors. Let dry.
Referring to the photo, *opposite,* paint stripes on
the ball. Let dry. Stencil stars where desired. Let
dry. When baseball is completely dry, wax the ball
and let dry. Buff the ball when necessary.

123

1 more idea...
Paint other desired motifs on
the baseball.

also try this...
Give the baseballs with rustic
candleholders to use as stands.

all-american flowerpot
make it in minutes

to make a
flowerpot you'll
need:

Newspapers
Red spray paint
Clay pot
Coarse red glitter,
  fine red glitter, and
  magenta glitter
Wood star
White paint pen
Adhesive-back
  silver hologram
  paper
Crafts knife
Silver cord
Scissors
Hot-glue gun
Hot-glue sticks

124

here's how

To make this flowerpot, use newspapers to cover the work surface in a well-ventilated work area. Spray-paint the clay pot red. Before drying, sprinkle the two red and the magenta glitters into wet paint. Let dry.

Paint the edge of the wood star with a white paint pen. Remove backing from silver hologram paper and apply to the wood star. Lay the star on a protected work surface, silver side down. Trim away the paper around the star using a crafts knife.

Hot-glue silver cording onto the pot, wrapping several times. Hot-glue the star onto the cord.

As dandy as a Fourth of July parade, these flowerpots will share your pride for America and make a welcoming summertime present.

1 more idea... •
Cover one side and the edges of the wood star with glue and sprinkle with silver glitter.

also try this... •
Decorate miniature flowerpots using this idea, fill them with sand, and use outdoors to hold sparklers in place.

spectacular

126

between friends

■ Honor the gift of friendship with crafts projects that acknowledge those special bonds. Choose the techniques you love most—decoupaging, painting, sewing, crocheting, candle making, glass painting, card making—and then get busy making best-friend gifts to be treasured forever.

dressy

peacock feather plate

make it in minutes

Share the breathtaking colors of a peacock feather by decoupaging it on a clear glass plate.

129

presentation

here's how

To make this project, wash and dry the plate thoroughly. Turn the plate over. Position the peacock feather on the plate and cut edges to fit. Remove the feather. Paint a layer of decoupage medium onto the back of the plate. Reposition the feather, adhering it to the plate. Carefully paint another layer of decoupage medium over the feather. Allow the plate to dry. Trim any edges of the feather that extend beyond the plate edge. Arrange candy on the plate.

to make the plate you'll need:
Clear glass plate with smooth bottom
Peacock feather
Scissors
Decoupage medium
Paintbrush
Purchased small chocolate candies

1 more idea...
Place favorite stickers on paper and cut out. Decoupage designs on the back of a clear glass plate.

For a coordinating wrap, place the plate in a box lined with shredded paper. Wrap the box with teal paper. Tie variegated ribbon across the middle of the box. Tuck two feathers under the ribbon. Add a gift tag if desired.

to make the wrap you'll need:
Box
Shredded paper
Teal wrapping paper
Variegated ribbon
Scissor
Peacock feather

also try this...
Photocopy old postcards and decoupage on the back of a glass tray.

pretty pails
step-by-step

to make a pail
you'll need:
Grease pencil
Aluminum, wood,
 or ceramic pail
Thick white crafts
 glue
Paintbrush
3-ply heavy cotton
 cord
Aluminum foil
Black India ink and
 brush
Scrub pad or #00
 steel wool
Newspapers
Gloss polyurethane
 spray

130

This rich faux metal relief method adds a designer
look to nearly any container.

Instructions on pages 132–133.

1 more idea...
Gild a wide picture frame
using aluminum foil and cord.

also try this...
To make circular designs, use
rubber washers.

giving

pretty pails (continued)

1 **Use a grease pencil** to draw simple designs on the pail.

2 **Working in one small section** at a time, squeeze glue on the pail following the drawn lines. Allow the glue to become tacky.

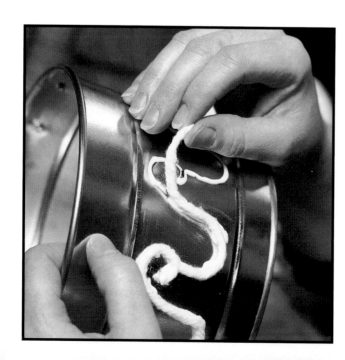

3 **Cut lengths of cord** to fit design and press pieces into glue. Continue working in this manner until the entire design is covered with cord. Let dry.

4 **Tear off a length of foil** long enough to go around the pail and overlap 6 inches. Cut the piece in half to make application easier. Set foil aside. Working on half of the pail, brush glue over the surface, including the cord. Gently crumple one piece of foil and lay over the glue-covered area. Press foil around the string and into the background. Trim foil so ¼ inch hangs over the top and bottom edges. Fold over edges of container. Repeat with remaining half and allow to dry.

5 **Paint over the foil** with ink, reapplying several times if needed to fill in all areas. Let the ink dry.

6 **Use a scrub pad** or steel wool to wipe off most of the ink, leaving ink in the crevices. In a well-ventilated work area, cover work surface with newspapers. Spray the pail with polyurethane. Let dry.

falling leaf candles
make it in minutes

to make a
candle you'll
need:
Pliable real or
   artificial leaves in
   autumn colors
Glue stick
White pillar candle
White taper candle

Here's an easy-to-make gift that will add to
an evening of enchantment.

presentation

134

here's how...

To make a candle, apply glue stick
to the back of each leaf. Press onto the
pillar candle for temporary adhesion. On
a protected work surface, lay the
candle carefully on its side. Light a white
taper candle and let the wax drip over
the leaves until all or mostly covered.
Let the wax cool and harden. Turn the
candle and repeat until all leaves are
embedded in wax.

**For a coordinating
wrap,** place a candle in a
box lined with tissue paper.
Wrap box with brown kraft
paper. Using a dried leaf as a
stamp, paint one side heavily
with ivory acrylic paint. Press
onto wrapping paper where
desired. Tie with a raffia bow.

to make the
wrap you'll
need:
Box
Tissue paper
Brown kraft paper
Scissors
Tape
Dried leaf
Ivory acrylic paint
Paintbrush
Natural raffia

1 more idea...
Embellish candles with green leaves or
pieces of fern for a brighter look.

also try this...
Use dried and pressed flowers instead
of leaves for a feminine touch.

meditate

enjoy

crocheted mats and rings

make it in minutes

Share your gift of crochet with these nifty tabletop accessories.

to make the mat you'll need:
1½ oz./42.5 g cotton 4-ply worsted-weight yarn—2 skeins of solid color, 3 skeins of multicolored yarn
Size J crochet hook
3 yards of 2¼-inch-wide ribbon

CROCHET ABBREVIATIONS	
ch	chain
dc	double crochet
hdc	half double crochet
lp(s)	loop(s)
rem	remaining
rep	repeat
sc	single crochet
sk	skip
sl st	slip stitch
sp	space
st(s)	stitch(es)
yo	yarn over

here's how

To make the mat, hold one strand of each yarn color together, chain 27. Sc in 2nd ch from hook, draw up a lp in same ch as first sc, draw up a lp in next ch, yo and draw through 3 lps on hook.* Draw up a lp in same ch as last st, draw up a lp in next ch, yo and draw through all 3 lps on hook; rep from * across—26 sts; turn.

Ch 1, sc in first st, draw up a lp in same st as first sc, draw up a lp in next sc, yo and draw through 3 lps on hook. * Draw up a lp in same st as last st, draw up a lp in next st, yo and draw through all 3 lps on hook; rep from * across; turn. Rep this row for 38 times more. Fasten off.

Join one strand of multicolored yarn with a sl st in right corner. In same sp as join, (sc, hdc, dc, hdc, sc—scallop made). Working along one short edge first, * sk next st, make a scallop in the next st; rep from * across to corner. For long edge, * sk 1 row, make a scallop in side of next row; rep from * to corner. Work rem sides as established. At end, join with a sl st in first sc and fasten off.

Beginning at top center, weave ribbon under and over every two crochet stitches one row in from edge. Tie ends into a bow.

here's how

To make the napkin ring, join cotton to ring with a sl st. Ch 1, work 32 sc around the ring. * Ch 3, sk 1 sc, sc in next sc; rep from * around. In each ch-3 sp work (sc, hdc, dc, hdc, sc). At end, join with sl st in first sc and fasten off.

to make the napkin ring you'll need:
1 skein #3 perle cotton
1½-inch-diameter plastic ring
Size 3 steel crochet hook

1 more idea...

Fold a place mat in half, weave ribbons up both sides, and secure for a little girl's purse.

also try this...

Make larger napkin rings and use as curtain tiebacks.

137

good ideas growing gifts

Crocus bulbs make a much-appreciated gift, and this presentation ushers even more compliments. Place the bulbs in a planter or long dish and surround the bulbs with marbles. Tie a sheer ribbon bow around the container. Give the blooms with planting instructions.

embellish

cheery sewing supplies

make it in minutes

to make the
scissors you'll
need:
Scissors with bright
  plastic handles
Rubbing alcohol
Disposable plate
Paint for plastic,
  such as Plaid, in
  desired colors
Paintbrushes
Sewing supplies
Small basket
Natural shredded
  paper

here's how

To make this project, wipe scissors handles with rubbing alcohol. Put a small dot of each paint color on a plate. Use colors that blend well together and complement the color of the handles. Decide where you want to place the designs. To make daisies, dip just the tip of the paintbrush into paint. Lightly touch the paint to the handle surface, making a tiny oval petal. Continue making petals in a circle, leaving the center open. Using white, highlight each petal. Make a tiny dot in the center using a different color of paint. Paint the stems and leaves using green highlighted with yellow. Allow the paint to dry for 48 hours before use. Arrange other sewing supplies around the scissors in shredded paper.

141

For anyone who loves to sew, this sewing
basket complete with painted scissors
offers a personalized set of tools.

1 more idea...
Personalize scissors by writing the recipient's
name on the handles using a paint marker.

also try this...
Paint butterflies, ladybugs, caterpillars, or
other simple designs on the handles of
children's scissors.

bow-tied basket liners
make it in minutes

142

here's how

To make a basket liner, measure the outside of the basket for width, length, and height as shown, *below*. For the main fabric measurement, add two times the height plus the width to equal the cutting width measurement; add two times the height plus the length to equal the cutting length measurement. Cut the fabric to this size.

For the liner, fold fabric on the bias. From one corner, measure the height. Mark and pin this point. Check the fit and make any necessary adjustments.

Stitch along bias from the mark at a right angle to the fold. Repeat for all four corners. Trim seam allowance to ¼ inch.

For the fold-over cuff, cut two pieces of contrasting fabric that each measure half the height plus half the circumference of the basket top. Cut

two pieces from the main fabric that are 1 inch wider.

Place a contrasting fabric piece over a main fabric piece with right sides facing. Stitch one long side on each pair using a ½-inch seam. Press.

Fold pieces lengthwise with right sides facing. Stitch across the ends. Trim the corners. Turn to the right side. If desired, stitch decorative trim over seam where fabrics meet. Baste the cuff from handle to handle with right sides facing. Stitch. Press cuff to right side. To make the fabric ties, cut two pieces 28×3½ inches. Fold lengthwise with right sides facing. Stitch, tapering to a point at ends and leaving an opening for turning. Turn. Stitch closed. Press. Tack ties to the sides of the liner. Form ties into bows.

Gift baskets are even more grand when lined with colorful fitted fabric.

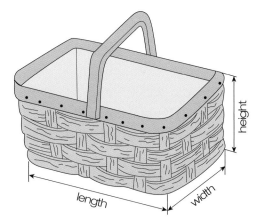

height

length

width

1 more idea...
Make a liner for a small square basket to use as a napkin holder.

also try this...
Purchase enough fabric to make a coordinating picnic tablecloth.

soften

143

good ideas celebration glassware

Here's a simple gift to make using strokes of paint.
Choose candleholders or candy jars and use glass
paint to add free-form or detailed designs. Follow
the paint manufacturer's painting recommendations
for applying and curing the paint.

sweet perfume

dainty potpourri box

to make the
box you'll need:
Crayola Model
  Magic clay
Rolling pin
Small heart cookie
  cutter
Butter knife
Thick white crafts
  glue
Round box with lid
  approximately
  6 inches in
  diameter and
  3½ inches high
Acrylic paints
  in white,
  red, green,
  pale and
  bright yellow,
  and blue
Fine-point
  and
  small flat
  paintbrushes
White gel stain
Damp, soft cloth
Potpourri

This beautiful gift box, holding fresh
floral scents, is accented with
painted clay shapes.

1 **Roll out clay** to a thickness of approximately ³⁄₁₆ inch. Cut out four
small hearts with cookie cutter. Set aside to dry.

2 **Shape each leaf** by forming a marble-size ball out of clay. Flatten
it into an oval shape and press a crease into the center with the blade of
a knife.

3 **Form seven or eight small balls** to place in the center of the
flower. To make the blue flowers around the edge, form five balls of clay
for each flower. Shape tiny leaves out of clay. Let shapes dry.

4 **Glue clay shapes** onto the lid and sides of the box.

Instructions continue on pages 148–149.

1 more idea...
Use Christmas cookie
cutters to make gift boxes
for the holidays.

also try this...
Decorate the lid of a
plain photo storage box
using this method.

dainty potpourri box (continued)

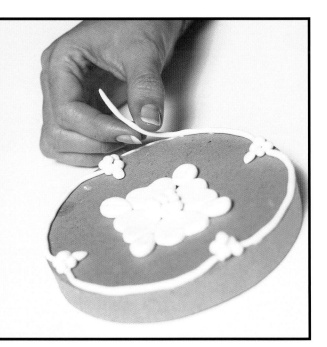

5 **Coil a piece of clay** into a ⅛-inch-thick rope to trim the edge of lid. Place a thin line of glue around the edge and add the rope of clay around the edge, meeting at each flower. Let the clay dry on the box.

6 **Paint the entire box,** inside and out, using white. Let the paint dry. Paint pale yellow over the white. Slightly overlap the paint onto the flowers and rope. Let the paint dry. Paint the large flowers red, the leaves and rope green, the small flowers blue, and all the flower centers bright yellow. Let the paint dry.

7 **Coat the entire outside** of the box and the lid using a generous amount of white gel stain. Brush the gel stain into all of the crevices of the clay design.

8 **Let the gel just begin to dry** and gently wipe off with the damp, soft cloth. Wipe off just enough to remove the top surface, leaving the white stain in the crevices. Let the stain dry.

9 **Fill the box** with your choice of purchased or homemade potpourri.

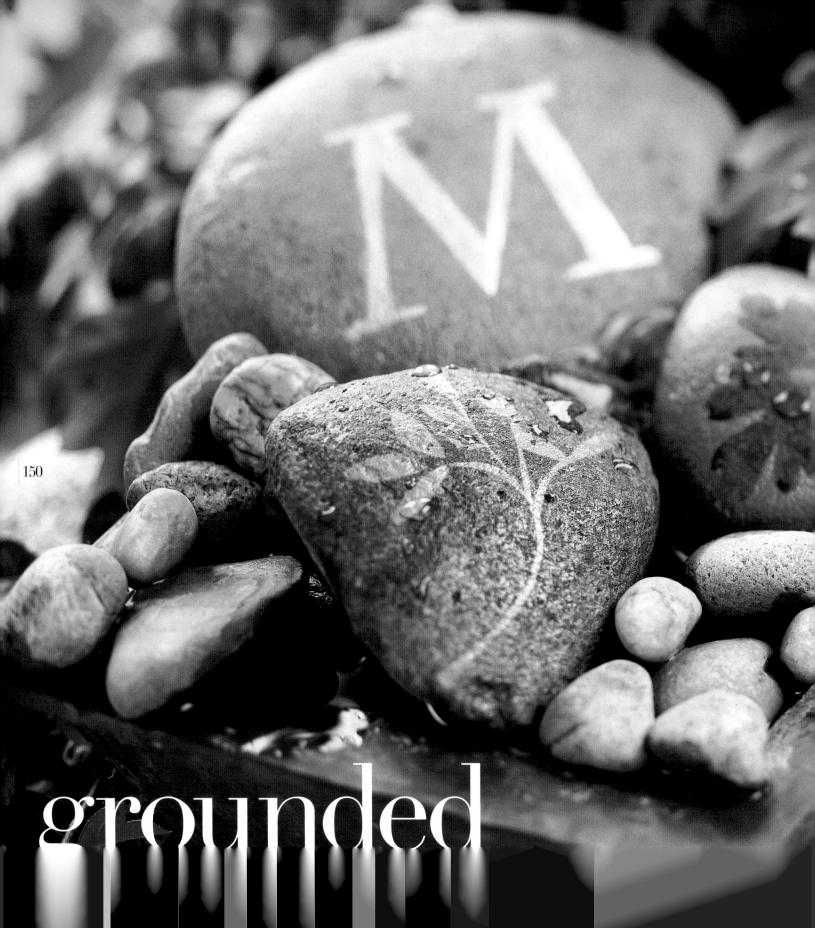

grounded

garden gems

make it in minutes

to make these
rocks you'll
need:

Rocks with smooth
  surfaces
Leaves
Alphabet stencil
Heavy paper
Pencil
Crafts knife
Spray adhesive
Newspapers
Spray paint in gold,
  copper, or other
  desired color

here's how

To make a rock, wash
and dry it if necessary.

For the painted leaf or initial
designs, trace a leaf or letter
in the center of a piece of
heavy paper. Using a crafts
knife, cut along the traced
lines, remove the shape, and
discard leaving a stencil.
Spray the back side of paper
leaf or alphabet cutout with
spray adhesive.

For the painted rock, spray
back side of leaves with
adhesive. Place onto rock.

For both rocks, cover work
surface with newspapers in a
well-ventilated work area.
Spray rocks with three light
coats of spray paint. Let
dry. Remove leaves or
paper stencil.

151

Give a gift that can be used indoors or out—
rocks with a personal touch.

1 more idea...
Make enough monogrammed rocks to
spell a name or *Welcome*.

also try this...
Use bright-colored spray paints for
someone with contemporary tastes.

good wish greetings
step-by-step

to make a
dragonfly card
you'll need:

Scissors
Paper in green,
  purple, and white
Decorative-edge
  scissors
Thick white crafts
  glue
Narrow leaves
Twigs
White spray primer
Newspapers
Allspice or any small
  ball shape
Acrylic paints in
  green and purple
Fine liner paintbrush
White glitter
  tube-style paint

152

Nature inspired, these handmade
greeting cards are sure to
touch the heart.

DRAGONFLY CARD (opposite, upper right)

1 **Fold and cut each paper** to create a card of successively wider layers. The narrower outside layer should be purple, and the wider inside layer should be green. Trim the edges with decorative-edge scissors as desired. Put one dab of glue on the back half of each layer and press to next layer to adhere.

2 **In a well-ventilated work area,** cover the work surface with newspapers. Prime the leaves and twigs with white spray primer. Let dry.

3 **Paint narrow leaves, allspice, and twigs** green. Paint purple dots on twigs. Let dry.

4 **Glue the leaves, allspice, and twigs in place** to form a dragonfly.

5 **Use a glitter paint** to draw swirls.

Instructions continue on pages 154–155.

1 more idea... ●
Arrange the leaves as flower petals and
paint with colorful tones.

also try this... ●
For kids' cards, make bug eyes by
sewing on white seed beads with
French knot centers made of black
embroidery floss.

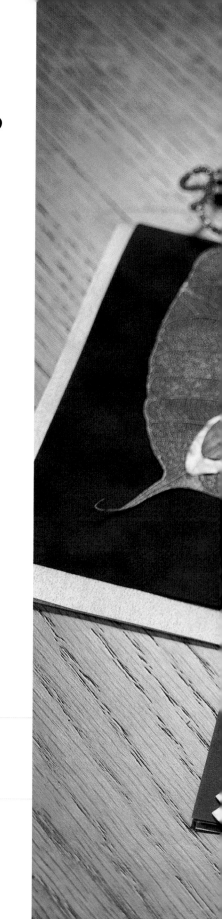

natural

good wish greetings (continued)

for the purple
butterfly you'll
need:
Waxed paper
White spray primer
Leaves
Twig
Pine needles
Metallic acrylic
  paints in purple
  and turquoise
Medium paintbrush
Paper in gold,
  white, and purple
Scissors
Decorative-edge
  scissors
Thick white crafts
  glue
Coordinating velour
  yarn

154

PURPLE BUTTERFLY (lower left, *page 153*)

1 **In a well-ventilated work area,** cover the work surface with
waxed paper Spray primer on the leaves. Let dry. Paint one edge of the
leaves purple and the other turquoise as shown *above*. Wipe off excess
paint from the brush and blend the two wet colors together in the middle.
Paint the twig and pine needles purple. Paint turquoise dots on the twig.

2 **Fold and cut the papers** to create a layered card. Trim the
edges with decorative scissors as desired. Layer the folded papers,
placing a small dab of glue on the back half of top two layers to adhere.

3 **Use a small dab of glue** on the back of leaves, twig, and pine
needles to attach to the front of the card.

4 **Tie the layers together** at the fold with a piece of decorative
velour yarn.

GOLDEN BUTTERFLY (top left, *page 153*)

1 **Paint large leaves gold** and let dry. If necessary, apply a second coat of paint. Let dry. Paint the smaller leaves in different colors as shown, using green, turquoise, and magenta. Add a tiny gold dot on the magenta leaf. Let dry.

2 **Prepare a card** to fit the size of your butterfly. Cut the translucent gold layer a little larger than the purple velour layer. Fold the layers.

3 **In a well-ventilated work area,** cover work surface with newspapers. Lightly spray back of gold leaves with adhesive. Let dry a bit. Spray light coats until the surface is quite tacky and covered well with adhesive. Be sure to hold the spray can a good distance from the leaf and allow time to dry between light coats. The leaves require a little extra adhesive because they will be attached to velour paper. Place the gold leaves in position on the purple layer. Press firmly in place.

4 **Glue the green leaves** in place using crafts glue. Layer and glue the magenta and turquoise leaves using crafts glue and then glue onto the green leaves.

5 **Tie a pony bead** on one end of a wire. String on a magenta bead, about 2½ inches of gold seed beads, and a length of pony beads to form the body of the butterfly. Poke a tiny hole through both layers of paper at the bottom of the butterfly and insert the beaded wire through the hole from the front side of the card to the inside; pull the wire to the top of the butterfly body and poke back through to the front side. Keeping the wire pulled tight, string on another 2½ inches of gold seed beads, a magenta bead, and one last pony bead. Firmly pull the wire back through the magenta bead and several other beads. Twist the two beaded wire ends together at the base of the gold seed beads.

for the golden butterfly you'll need:

Leaves in assorted sizes
Metallic acrylic paints in golden yellow, lime green, turquoise, and magenta
Medium and small paintbrushes
Purple velour paper
Translucent gold paper
Scissors
Newspapers
Spray adhesive
White spray primer
Thick white crafts glue
24-inch-long piece of beading wire
Gold seed beads
2 magenta beads
Iridescent pony beads
24-inch-long piece of fine wire

night out

156

dinner napkin purses

make it in minutes

157

here's how

To make the vertical purple and gold purse, fold the napkin in half, right side out. The folded edge will become the top of the purse. Fold the napkin in thirds menu-style, then tuck one napkin end inside the other.

For the green and cream purse, fold napkin in thirds menu style. The open flap will fall along the bottom edge of the purse. Fold the napkin in thirds again. Tuck one napkin end inside the other.

To finish the above purses, cut the beaded fringe to span the bottom edge of the purse. Tuck the binding of the fringe up inside the bottom of the purse and then pin the bottom edge closed. Use the needle and thread to stitch the side and bottom edge closed. Sew a snap to the inside top of the purse. Cut a 7-inch-long piece of wire and then loop one end into a circle. Thread the wire with beads and then loop the other end. Position the looped handle ends inside the bag and then stitch them in place.

For the gold-on-gold envelope purse, fold the napkin in thirds, right side facing out. Fold the bottom open end of the napkin up 4 to 5 inches (just over two thirds of the way) and then pin the sides together. Use the needle and thread to stitch the sides closed. Cut the beaded fringe to span the top edge. Tuck the fringe binding down into the top of the napkin, pin, and stitch the top edge closed. Fold the top flap down over the purse. Stitch one side of the snap to the underside of the top flap and the other side onto the top of the purse.

to make a purse you'll need:

New full-size dinner napkin
1-foot length of beaded fringe per purse
Needle and matching thread
Straight pins
Matching beads (for the handle)
Sew-on snap
24-gauge wire

These elegant little bags are the perfect surprise for any sociable gal.

1 more idea...
Pin a chic brooch on the purse for two gifts in one.

also try this...
Pick up necklaces at flea markets and use the beads to make purse fringe.

pretty essential

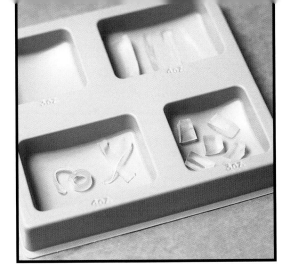

geometric soaps

step-by-step

to make the
soap you'll
need:
Blocks of
   translucent
   (glycerin) soap in
   pink, blue, and
   green (available
   at crafts stores)
Block of opaque
   white soap
   (available at
   crafts stores)
Sharp knife
Glass container for
   melting soap
Toothpick
Purchased soap
   mold, deep
   plastic cookie
   cutter, or desired
   mold shape
Aluminum foil

159

2 **For striped or X and O soap,** follow directions as for checkerboard soap, except cut strips of pink or a pink X and green O and lay in the bottom of the mold as shown, *left*.

1 **To make checkerboard soap,** cut a ⅜-inch slice of the pink soap. Cut that slice into nine cubes. Arrange five of the cubes in the bottom of the mold as shown, *above*. Set aside. Cube the white soap into the glass container. Melt in the microwave until just melted. Remove and let set until a film forms over the top. Push the film away with a toothpick and carefully pour the white soap into the mold over the pink soap. Let it set for a few minutes. Arrange the last four cubes of pink soap in openings between the first pink soap cubes. Finish filling the mold. Allow to cool thoroughly before removing from mold.

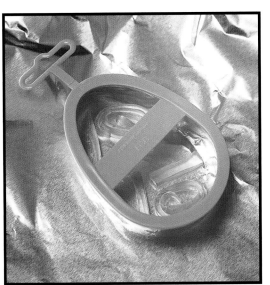

3 **For the egg soap,** place egg cookie cutter on a sheet of foil. Arrange shapes of soap on the foil as shown, *left*. Slowly fill with white melted soap. Allow to cool. Remove soap from the cookie cutter.

A wonderful addition to a basket, this pretty pastel soap is the perfect springtime gift.

presentation

For an easy and elegant gift wrap, fill a glass dish with shredded paper. Place soap in the center of the dish. Tie with a wired ribbon bow.

1 more idea...
For parents with a newborn, place a rubber duck or small rattle in a bar of soap.

also try this...
Paint solid-color soap holders to coordinate with soap.

good ideas | de-lightful gifts

Candlelight is lovely when it
bounces off clear glass.
Here candles float in dishes
that reflect the candle's
shape. Tied with ribbon
bows, these clever gifts are
sure to light the way to a
friend's heart.

sunshine planter
step-by-step

to make the
planter you'll
need:

Glass bowl with
 straight sides
¾-inch masking
 tape
Etching cream
Paintbrushes
Rubber gloves
Glass paints in
 yellow, green,
 white, and blue

162

Etching cream and glass paints
add a cheery touch to this versatile
container, which can be
used as a planter or candy dish—
the perfect gift for a best friend.

Instructions are on pages 164–165.

1 more idea...
Create a checkerboard effect by placing
square pieces of masking tape on the
glass surface before etching.

also try this...
Paint only on the outside of
the bowl and use as a
serving piece for food.

cheerful

sunshine planter (continued)

1 **Cut and place pieces** of masking tape vertically on bowl, allowing ¾ inch between each piece. Continue until masking tape pieces are pressed securely around entire bowl.

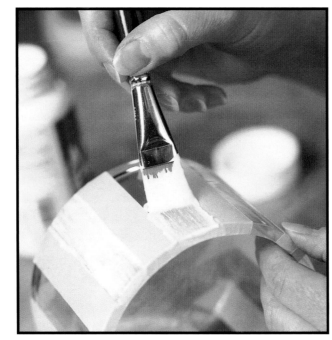

2 **Paint etching cream** between masking tape pieces. Follow the manufacturer's directions.

3 **Wearing gloves,** wash off the etching cream and remove the tape. Dry the bowl.

4 **On the inside of the bowl,** paint yellow stripes between the etched stripes. Paint flower stems (elongated, backward S's) on the inside of the bowl behind the etched stripes.

5 **On the outside of the bowl,** paint flowers and dots as desired. To paint dots, dip the handle of a paintbrush into paint and dot onto the surface. Let the paint dry. Bake the glass bowl in the oven if recommended by the paint manufacturer.

Note: For a planter, be sure to use a plastic liner before potting the plant.

very special occasions

■ Send thoughtful congratulatory wishes with these clever wedding, baby, and housewarming gifts. While store-bought gifts may be quickly forgotten, these make-it-yourself beauties will be long remembered.

"I do" duo
make it in minutes

to make the wedding pitcher and goblets you'll need:
Glass pitcher
Goblets
Wired beads or pearls
Pearl jewelry, appliqués, or buttons
Wire cutter
Tacky putty, such as type used for bulletin boards

here's how

To make this project, begin with clean, dry glass. Wind pearls or beads around goblets and pitcher in a random manner. If using jewelry pins or earrings, clip the backs off using wire cutter. Position the pieces using the tacky putty. This medium is temporary and can be removed or reapplied easily.

168

fold   fold   fold

For a coordinating wrap, cushion glassware in shredded paper and place in a box. Wrap box with pastel paper. Wrap package as desired with pearls. Hot-glue in place. Trace pattern, *left*, on tracing paper. Cut out. Fold a piece of decorative white paper. Trace around pattern on paper, aligning folds. Cut out. Hot-glue heart tag to gift.

Dripping with wedding-white pearls,

this frilly set will be used for many an anniversary.

1 more idea...
Decorate a bottle of champagne using wired beads and assorted trims.

also try this...
Personalize the glassware by using purchased lace or embroidered initials.

wedded bliss

anniversary wishes
make it in minutes

to make a card you'll need:

Purchased note cards

Black and white photocopy of the happy couple

Colored pencils, such as Prismacolors

Art papers and/or vellum

Thick white crafts glue

Glue stick

Small quantities of fabrics or trims to match the anniversary year *(see list, right)*

here's how

To make a card, cut a rectangle of the desired fabric and glue it to the center front of the card cover.

Use a color photograph as a guide to hand-color the photocopy. Make loose diagonal strokes with the colored pencils. Use warm skin tones to enliven the black and white photocopy.

Crop the colored photo and mount it to the center of the note card over the fabric. Hot-glue the desired trim to the edge of the photocopy. Fold a matching art paper or vellum sheet in half, and trim it to fit inside the card.

To secure the paper/vellum inside the card, make a large stitch with thin ribbon through all layers of the paper along the folded edge of the card. Tie the ribbon ends into a bow.

YEAR	TRADITIONAL	MODERN
First	Paper	Clocks
Second	Cotton	China
Third	Leather	Crystal, Glass
Fourth	Flowers	Electrical Appliances
Fifth	Wood	Silverware
Sixth	Candy, Iron	Wood
Seventh	Copper, Wool	Desk Sets
Eighth	Bronze, Pottery	Linens
Ninth	Pottery, Willow	Leather
Tenth	Tin, Aluminum	Diamond Jewelry
Eleventh	Steel	Fashion Jewelry
Twelfth	Silk, Linen	Pearl
Thirteenth	Lace	Textiles, Furs
Fourteenth	Ivory	Gold Jewelry
Fifteenth	Crystal	Watches
Twentieth	China	Platinum
Twenty-fifth	Silver	Silver
Thirtieth	Pearl	Diamond
Thirty-fifth	Coral	Jade
Fortieth	Ruby	Ruby
Forty-fifth	Sapphire	Sapphire
Fiftieth	Gold	Gold
Fifty-fifth	Emerald	Emerald
Sixtieth	Diamond	Diamond
Seventy-fifth	Diamond	Diamond

Sweetly acknowledge the celebration of an anniversary with a card they will never forget.

1 more idea...
Hand-letter the couple's names and wedding date to customize your card.

also try this...
Look for small charms (gold rings, hearts, etc.) to string to the ribbon on the front.

congratulate

172

remembrance

wedding ornament
make it in minutes

to make the
ornament you'll
need:
Round pink glass
    ornament
White wedding trim
    (available at fabric
    and crafts stores)
Thick white crafts
    glue
Pearls on filament
Scissors
Beaded wire
White garland
Crystal dish

here's how

To make an ornament, decide on placement for the wedding trim. Glue the trim in place. Cut 3-inch lengths of pearls on filament. Glue to ornament, tucking ends behind the trim piece. Let the glue dry. Thread beaded wire through the ornament hanger. Curl the wire ends or twist together if hanging. To present as a gift, place the ornament in a bed of white garland nestled in the bottom of a crystal dish.

173

Add to the newlyweds' holiday collection with a sparkling ornament reminiscent of their big day.

1 more idea...
Glue clear rhinestones to the ornament for added sparkle.

also try this...
Write the wedding date on the bottom of the ornament using white paint pen.

enveloped

lingerie bag
make it in minutes

to make this bag you'll need:
Place mat, approximately 14×19 inches, that features two borders of eyelet edging
4mm silk embroidery ribbon in pale yellow
7mm silk embroidery ribbon in coral and yellow-green
1-inch-wide taupe grosgrain ribbon
1½-inch sew-through pearl button
1-inch ceramic bird button

Here's the perfect project for the nonsewer—
a dainty fabric envelope that's woven at the sides.

here's how

To make a bag, work the inside eyelet area with pale yellow ribbon, weaving in and out every other hole. Work coral silk ribbon in zigzags, through every other yellow weave, leaving small loops.

Fold place mat with wrong sides facing; match the eyelets on the bottom 6¼ inches to form an envelope. Pin the sides together along the outside eyelets. Hand-tack the end of the

yellow-green silk ribbon to secure it in place. Weave it in and out of double layers to lace the bag together. Repeat for opposite side. Work a single layer of weaving for flap.

Seam the ends of the taupe ribbon. Gather along one edge, pulling tight to secure into circle. Center gathered ribbon at the lower edge of flap. Sew bird button and pearl button stacked through the center of the gathers.

1 more idea...
To personalize the bag, use an initial brooch in place of the buttons.

also try this...
Weave silk ribbons through openings in a tablecloth for added embellishment.

picture it

PHOTOS

beautiful brag book

make it in minutes

Give proud new parents
the gift they'll love sharing—
an accordion-folded book
that protects photos of
their little angel.

● *1 more idea...*
Make smaller versions of the
book to display school photos.

● *also try this...*
Make interesting tissue paper by stamping
it before applying to cardboard pieces.

here's how

To make this book, cut tissue into sixteen 9-inch squares. Crumple the tissue squares into a ball and then open up and smooth out.

Pour glue into pie pan. Add enough water to make it the consistency of heavy cream. With the paintbrush, brush one side of six poster board squares with the glue. Lay tissue square over board. Place a piece of waxed paper over tissue and rub across the tissue with your fist to seal it to the board. Set aside to dry. Glue tissue to the other side of the six boards in the same manner. Using the glue/water mixture, adhere tissue only to one side of the remaining two boards. Let dry.

Trim away excess tissue. Using the glue/water mixture, adhere tissue to one side of each of the mat board squares, and trim off excess. Glue the back side of the mat board squares to the back of the last two poster board squares, making sure the tissue paper sides are facing out.

To join the squares, begin by placing two poster boards back to back. To create a hinge, wrap an adhesive label over the edges of the two squares, centering the label as much as possible along the edge. Open the squares up and turn them over. Using the location of the label on the first side, place a label in the same position on this side. Continue to add a square at a time in the same manner until all six squares are joined in a line.

Add each end of the line of squares to the back of a mat board square. Add a label to the opposite edge of the mat board for balance. Accordion-pleat the squares to fit between the two mat board covers. Add a label perpendicular to the label on the right side of the cover. Apply adhesive letters within this label to spell *photos*. Cover the ¾-inch strip of poster board with tissue and trim away the excess. When dry, wrap the strip around the book. Where the edges of the strip overlap, cut a slit in each side, on the opposite edge from each other. Interlock the strip together at these slits. Bend the ends of the strip back flat.

to make the book you'll need:
Scissors
Tissue paper in a
    variety of pastel
    colors
White glue
Metal pie pan
Flat paintbrush
Poster board—
    enough for eight
    7-inch squares
    and a ¾x18-inch
    strip
Waxed paper
Mat board—
    enough for two
    7-inch squares
1x2-inch adhesive
    labels
¾-inch gold
    adhesive
    letters

177

good ideas bonded booties

Soft baby booties are always a welcome gift for a new arrival. To make the gift truly unforgettable, tuck in a savings bond as the first contribution toward the child's college fund. Pair the goodies with a children's storybook to complete the presentation.

remember

sweet baby books

make it in minutes

Dainty designs on soft felt are the perfect combination for creating a memory book for a new baby.

1 more idea...
Stitch the baby's name below the moon or star.

also try this...
Make a book in primary colors for moms and dads who like vivid tones.

here's how

To make one of these books, cut a 7x11¾-inch piece of felt to cover the front and back of the album and two 3x7-inch rectangles of felt for the front and back inside cover flaps. To cover a larger or smaller album, make a pattern by laying the covers and center spine flat on a piece of paper. Trace around the covers and then add ⅛ inch to all sides before cutting out the felt. Use the length of the cover to determine the length of the two inside cover flaps. Adjust the width of the flaps to fit your album (3 inches in width is a good starting point).

Draw a simple star or moon or trace a cookie cutter on white felt. Cut out shape. Arrange the pattern pieces on the center of the right half of the precut felt cover. Working with one pattern piece at a time, stitch them in place. To stitch the small stars, start with a single horizontal white or silver stitch and then layer two diagonal and one vertical stitch over the center of the first stitch.

Use the white thread to stitch pearl eyes and accents onto the pattern pieces. With several strands of the white floss, stitch a small mouth on the star or moon and then stitch a lettered message. Position the flaps under the right- and left-hand edges of the cover. Working with one side and flap at a time, blanket-stitch (see *page 85*) the outer edge of the flap to the outer edge of the cover. Repeat the process to attach the second flap to the opposite side of the cover. Slip each album cover into the finished flaps.

to make a book you'll need:
Stiffened felt in blue or pink and white (available in crafts and fabric stores)
Scissors
Album, approximately 5¼x6¾ inches with a ¾-inch-wide spine
Matching blue or pink, white, and silver embroidery floss
Darning needle
Pearl beads
Star or moon cookie cutter, optional
Pencil

181

front door vase

make it in minutes

To make the vase you'll need:

Pencil
Tin snips
Work gloves
2 feet of wire window screen
Marking pen
½-inch-wide fabric adhesive first-aid tape
Wooden spoon
Newspapers
Spray paint in gold and cherry wood tones
Paper clip
Fine crafts wire
5 feet of 6-gauge copper wire
Large bead
Artificial leaves
Hot-glue gun
Hot-glue sticks
Needlenose pliers

here's how

To make this project, draw a 24-inch circle on screen. Wearing gloves, cut out circle. Make a cut from the outside edge to center. Shape screen into a cone; trim away excess. Open up screen. Encase cut edges of screen with cloth tape. Rub with spoon.

In a well-ventilated work area, cover work surface with newspapers. Spray-paint both sides of the screen with cherry wood tone paint. Let dry. With curved edge at top, roll screen into a cone shape. Overlap straight edges slightly, and clip top edges together with a paper clip. Cut small lengths of wire, fold in half, and insert through overlapped area. Twist ends together. Repeat every inch to secure cone shape. Remove paper clip.

Spray artificial leaves gold. Let dry. Glue leaves around top of cone. Wire large bead to tip. Using needle-nose pliers, twist one end of the copper wire into a small loop. With hands, twist wire into flat concentric circles around loop. Leave the last 8 inches at the end straight. Pull spiral up so the circles spread apart to form a cone. Insert screen cone and adjust wire to fit. Bend 4 inches of the top out to a 45-degree angle. Use pliers to shape wire into a circle for a hanger. Fill cone as desired.

presentation

For a coordinating wrap, place vase in a box cushioned with shredded paper. Wrap box in wrapping paper with gold accents. Tie package with gold screen-like ribbon or strips of fiberglass screen spray-painted gold. Hot-glue metallic gold leaves where ribbons intersect. Add a gift tag if desired.

Filled with best wishes and housewarming sentiments, this striking vase is made of window screen and copper wire.

1 more idea... ●
String small glass beads on thin wire and wrap around copper wire before shaping.

also try this... ●
Add a beaded tassel to the bottom point of the cone.

welcome

183

autumnal

Bring this fall centerpiece to a
new neighbor to make a
lasting first impression.

fall centerpiece

step-by-step

to make the
centerpiece
you'll need:
Pedestal dish
Silk leaves and
  flowers
Hot-glue gun
Hot-glue sticks
Moss
Pumpkin
Artificial berries on
  stems

1 To cover the pedestal dish, turn it over on work surface. Hot-glue leaves on the underside and pedestal of the dish.

2 Turn the pedestal dish right side up and hot-glue flowers around the base, in the center of the pedestal, and around the rim.

3 Fill the dish with moss. Place a pumpkin in the center of the dish. Tuck in stems of berries on each side of the pumpkin.

185

1 more idea...
Use this technique to adorn baskets and flowerpots.

also try this...
Use dried flowers to enhance a pedestal dish holding artificial fruit.

A Gift for You

teacher's pet

blackboard tins

make it in minutes

Bring the teacher a gift with classroom charm—flea market trays and tins painted with ready-for-chalk blackboard paint.

to make the tin and tray you'll need:
Tin trays, silver-plated trays, or cookie tins
Fine-grit sandpaper
Sponge paintbrush
Chalkboard paint (available in paint, art, and crafts stores)
White chalk
Acrylic paints in desired colors
Paintbrushes
Soft rag
Satin sealer, such as Varathane

here's how

To make this project, clean the tray and/or tin with soap and water. Let the items dry. Lightly sand the surface of the tray or tin top.

Using the sponge paintbrush, paint top of tray with one coat of chalkboard paint, painting in one direction. Let dry and paint with a second coat. Let dry.

Use the white chalk to add stripes, dots, and other designs around the edge of the tray. Paint over the chalk lines with acrylic paint. Let dry.

Wipe off any visible chalk with a rag. Paint the designed area with sealer, avoiding the center of the tray.

1 more idea...

Transform a frame into a mini memo board with a chalkboard-painted insert.

also try this...

To create a built-in memo board, tape off an area on a wall and fill in with chalkboard paint. Paint colorful freehand flowers around the masked area.

good ideas appreciation apples

Students can be the apple of their teacher's eye with this clever presentation. Shine up a bright red apple and set it in a clear glass apple dish. Use a long length of plaid ribbon to hold the apple in place in the dish. Tie the ribbon ends into a generous bow, securing to the apple stem.

Black eyed Susan

Forget me not

Hollyhock

190

Pansy

Kale

earthly

Squash

Beet

green-thumb plant pokes

make it in minutes

to make the
plant pokes you
will need:
2×2-inch tiles
Isopropyl alcohol
Pencil
Small paintbrush
Glass or ceramic
   paints in ochre,
   brown, light and
   dark green, light
   purple, and blue
Disposable plates
Tile adhesive
Cedar shims

here's how

To make a plant poke, wash a tile with soap and water. Rinse the tile and pat dry. Brush a coat of alcohol over the tiles to remove any remaining oils, such as fingerprints. Let the tiles air-dry.

Using the photograph, *opposite,* as inspiration, draw a simple flower or vegetable on the tile. Mix small quantities of two paint colors together, each mixed on a separate plate. For a lighter color, dilute the paint with a drop of water.

Paint the designs as desired. Allow the paint to dry 24 hours and then follow package directions to bake the painted tiles in the oven. Let the tiles cool. Use tile adhesive to attach the wide end of a cedar shim to the back of each tile.

191

Tiny tiles, available in a rainbow of colors,
      are ready-made canvases for painted plant
pokes—perfect for any garden lover.

1 more idea...
Paint large tiles to add interest to
a walking path or garden.

also try this...
Let kids paint small tiles to brighten
up indoor plants.

good ideas secretary's gift

Send a word of thanks your secretary's way with paint pen messages and designs on colorful bottles. Add a fresh-picked bloom or two and your office help won't stop thanking you.

music vase
make it in minutes

Music lovers
will sing your praises
when you present
them with
this striking vase.

194

here's how

To make a vase, roll out an 18-inch-long piece of tape on a cutting board. From the length cut five strips, each ³⁄₁₆ inch wide. Discard remaining strip.

Using the photograph, *opposite,* as a guide for the music staff, position one tape strip across the vase front at an upward angle. Continue the tape on the right side of the vase. Place another piece of tape ⅝ inch from the first piece of tape. Continue adding tape strips in this manner until you've placed five narrow masking tape lines with a ⅝-inch space between each piece of tape.

In a well-ventilated work area, cover surface with newspapers. Spray a light coat of white pearl spray paint on vase. Paint a second light coat if needed, preserving the transparent appearance.

Trace the patterns, *left.* Tape the pattern to the inside of the vase. Draw over the pattern with hot-glue gun using a silver glue stick.

Draw notes randomly, applying a generous dab of silver glue to the base of each note. While the glue is wet, press a flat marble in place. Let dry.

1 more idea... ●
Use etching cream as an alternative to the spray paint.

also try this... ●
Metallic paint pens and permanent markers can replace the silver glue.

harmonious

clever wraps & bows

Make the wrap as special as the gift itself with extraordinary papers, tags, and toppers. This chapter offers clever hand-painted gift wrap, personalized cans, ooh-la-la bows, and oodles of bright and cheerful gift bags to give your handcrafted treasures the wonderful wraps they deserve.

personalize

personally yours

make it in minutes

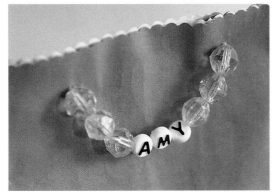

here's how

To make a can, drill a hole into each side of the can at the top. To make the handle, bend wire around a pencil approximately five times. Place a bead on the wire. Bend the wire around a pencil again. Repeat until the desired length is achieved. Attach the wire to the can. Thread desired alphabet beads onto a double strand of floss.

Make a knot on each side of the row of beads. Tie floss onto handle on each side so beads drape down. Glue pieces of ribbon and rickrack around the can.

To make a bag, place the gift in bag. Thread beads on floss and sew onto bag. Knot in back.

To wrap a box, wrap ribbon around box and secure in back with tape. Thread beads on narrow ribbon and layer over ribbon. Knot ribbon ends together on the back of the package.

Here's a playful touch that makes everyone feel special: their name spelled out in beads.

● *1 more idea...*
For two gifts in one, make an alphabet-bead necklace to hang around a package.

● *also try this...*
Use beads to spell out a phrase, such as *Happy Birthday, Congratulations Graduate,* or *Good for You!*

good ideas jingle bell wrap

Add a little jingle to holiday packages with this last-minute addition. Thread a large-eyed needle with raffia, embroidery floss, or thin ribbon. Fold over the top lip of a gift bag and sew across the bag to close, attaching jingle bells as you go. (If needed, pre-punch holes using a small paper punch.) Tie a bow with the raffia ends.

fancy-flap sacks
make it in minutes

From so-so to wow, these bright colored gift sacks grab attention with just a few stitches and trims.

202

here's how

To make a sack, place your gift inside the sack. Thread embroidery floss on a needle, using all six strands. Using the photograph, *opposite,* for ideas, plan the top of the bag. You can leave the top up or fold it down into a flap. Glue on rickrack trim where desired. Add decorative stitches, such as oversize cross-stitches and running stitches. Sew on buttons with floss, leaving the floss ends exposed to knot on top of the buttons.

1 more idea...
For the envelope-style bag, use adhesive Velcro to secure the flap down.

also try this...
Make a hugs and kisses bag by combining large cross-stitches and round buttons.

closure

polished wrap
make it in minutes

After you're done painting your nails, keep the bottle handy
to pretty-up some wrapping paper with freehand flowers.

here's how

To make the wrap, cut two pieces
of red wrapping paper, one large
enough to wrap the lid, the other large
enough to wrap the box.

For the lid paper, use fingernail polish
to paint a design. For each color, make
two short, curved lines side by side.
Continue adding motifs until the paper is
covered. Let dry. Add two silver lines
perpendicular to the fingernail polish lines.
Make three silver dots between motifs.

For the box paper, paint dime-size
circles using fingernail polish. Add flower
petals using a contrasting color. Paint
green stems and leaves. Let dry. Outline
flower centers using squiggly silver lines.
Make three silver dots between motifs.
Wrap lid and bottom.

For the bow, layer ribbons and tie a
bow. Thread beads on wire, securing
beads at each end. Wrap beaded wire
around the center of bow. Twist ends to
secure. Hot-glue to package top. Add a
tag if desired.

1 more idea...
For a lighthearted approach,
trace your hand and paint
colorful fingernails.

also try this...
Use different color wrapping
papers to reflect the
sentiment and the season.

mulled spice bag
make it in minutes

Turn store-bought mulling spices into an even more personal gift with this dolled-up fabric pouch tied with simple cording and a decorative leaf.

to make the bag you'll need:
Scissors
Pinking shears
Ruler
Solid-color cotton fabric (one 10-inch square per bag)
Burlap or cotton mesh fabric (one 10-inch square per bag)
Sewing needle or large pin
Mulling spices (available at grocery stores and gourmet shops)
Yarn or cord
Cinnamon stick
Silver leaf (available at crafts and hobby stores)

205

here's how

To make this project, cut a 9-inch square out of solid-color cotton fabric using pinking shears. Cut a 9-inch square out of the mesh fabric using regular scissors. Fray the edges of the mesh fabric about ¾ inch by using a needle or large pin to loosen and remove threads around the perimeter. Lay the cotton square on top of the mesh square and pour about ⅓ cup of the mulling spices in the center. Draw the edges of the fabrics up around the spices and tie with yarn or cord to create a small bag. Slide a cinnamon stick and silver leaf behind the bow. Be sure to include the package directions for making mulled wine or cider.

● *1 more idea...*
Make potpourri bags using this quick and pretty packaging.

● *also try this...*
Replace the leaf with a sprig of artificial holly.

illuminating joy

stained glass sacks

make it in minutes

to make a sack you'll need:
Pencil
Tracing paper
Transfer paper
Purchased gift bag in desired color
Piece of cardboard to fit inside bag
Crafts knife
Small pieces of colored cellophane
Scissors
Thick white crafts glue

here's how

To make this project, trace the desired pattern, *left*. Using transfer paper, transfer the design to the front of the bag. Slide the small piece of cardboard inside the sack. Carefully cut out the pieces of the pattern using a crafts knife. Remove the cardboard. Lay the cellophane pieces over the cutout areas. Mark the cellophane to be cut just a little larger than the hole. Cut the cellophane. Put small dots of glue around the edges of the cellophane. Slide the cellophane inside the bag to fit around the hole. Repeat until all of the cellophane is in place. Allow to dry.

207

Make stained glass windows the easy way: place colored cellophane behind paper bag cutouts.

1 more idea...
For other holiday shapes, use cookie cutters as patterns.

also try this...
Outline the cutouts with glitter paint marker for added sparkle.

bejeweled

jewelry wraps
make it in minutes

Vintage floral brooches add a nostalgic
flair atop crossed ribbons.

to make this
wrap you'll
need:
Wrapping paper in
   a solid color or
   small print
Tape
Ribbon
Scissors
Brooch

here's how

To make this wrap, cover a gift box
with wrapping paper. Using a long
length of ribbon, place the center of the
ribbon vertically at the point where you
want the ribbons to intersect on the
front of the gift box. Bring the ribbon tails
around to the back of the package.
Twist once and bring the ribbon ends
horizontally around to the front. Knot
the ends and trim the tails if needed. Pin
a floral brooch to the knot in the ribbon.

209

1 more idea...
Attach a small framed photo to the
center of the ribbon.

also try this...
Clip or pin matching earrings above and
below the brooch.

basic bow
step-by-step

210

1 Fold ribbon back and, making strands approximately 7 inches long, or another desired length. Fold until there are three loops on each end.

2 After the final loop is made, bring the ribbon to the center of the bow and curl around in a loop in the center, leaving a tail hanging downward.

3 While still holding center loop in place, insert a pipe cleaner into the center loop and around to the back of the bow, tying in place.

4 Trim the ends at an angle and shape each bow loop uniformly.

add-a-trim topper
step-by-step

to make this
bow you'll need:
Spool of wide
   sheer wired
   ribbon
Scissors
Pipe cleaner or wire
Fine curling ribbon
Starfish or other
   desired
   decorative item
Hot-glue gun
Glue sticks

**2 Tie a pipe
cleaner** around
the center of the
loops to secure.

211

**1 Unwind the
ribbon** from the
spool so it is easy
to manipulate.
Begin gently
folding ribbon
back and forth,
making three
stacked loops,
each 7-inches
long, leaving a tail
on each end.

3 Tie several strands
of gold curling ribbon around
the center. Curl the ribbon
ends by holding the scissors
blade at an angle against the
ribbon and quickly pulling the
ribbons across the blade.

4 Hot-glue the starfish
or other decorative item in
the center of the bow.

**5 Shape the bow as
desired.** To trim the two tail
ends into a V shape, fold the
ribbon in half lengthwise and
cut from the outer edge
toward the fold at an angle.

sticker bow

step-by-step

1 **To trim the ribbon end** into a V shape, fold the ribbon in half lengthwise and cut from the outer edge toward the fold at an angle.

212

2 **Add glue to the package** where the ribbon will be placed. Lay down the ribbon, beginning at the bottom of the package, to the length you want it to be. Gently fold the ribbon back downward to three-fourths of the length of the ribbon, and add a dab of glue where you will crease and fold it backward again to form another but shorter loop. Bring back downward to the same creased spot, add another dab of glue, and fold back upward to make another, final loop. Trim the ribbon off at the creased spot.

3 **Affix a sticker** at the creased spot.

1 **Cut five strips** of 6½-inch-long ribbon for the flower center. Cut five strips of 8-inch-long ribbon for the outer portion of the flower. To cut each end into a V shape, fold the ribbon in half lengthwise and cut from the outer edge toward the fold at an angle.

2 **Stack the larger ribbons** on the bottom and the shorter ribbons centered on top. Tie with a fine wire.

petal topper
step-by-step

to make this
bow you'll need:
Two colors of
 grosgrain ribbon,
 each 1½ inches
 wide
Scissors
Fine wire
Large button
Colored floss for
 button

213

3 **Twist and spread** some of the ribbons apart. String a piece of floss through the button, and tie onto the center of the bow around to the back side of the bow.

4 **Continue spreading and twisting** the ribbons to make a uniform shape.

index

credits

Designers

Susan M. Banker
Pages 10–11, 36–37, 40–43, 52–55, 58–59, 64–65, 68–69, 78–81, 98–99, 120–121, 144–145, 162–165, 178–179, and 204.

Heidi Boyd
Pages 108–109, 156–157, 170–171, 180–181, and 190–191.

Donna Chesnut
Pages 34–35, 46–47, 50–51, 60–61, 66–67, 82–83, 86–87, 110–111, 117–119, and 160–161.

Carol Dahlstrom
Pages 12–13, 26–27, 30, 48–49, 60–61, 72–73, 100–103, 116, 128–129, 138–141, 158–159, 188–189, 192–193, and 206–209.

Phyllis Dunstan
Pages 28–29. 112–115, 130–133, 176–177, 182–183, and 186–187.

Amy Jorgensen
Pages 14–15 and 98–203.

Sandi Jorgensen
Pages 122–123.

Alexa Lett
Pages 20–21.

Kathy Moenkhaus
Pages 94–97.

Jill Severson
Pages 134–135.

Margaret Sindelar
Pages 16–17, 38–39. 70–71, 76–77, 84–85, 88–89, 136–137, 142–143, and 172–175.

Alice Wetzel
Pages 18–19, 22–25. 32–33, 56–57, 74–75, 90–93, 104–107, 124–125, 134, 146–155, 168–169, 172–173, 185–185, and 194–195.

Photostyling

Carol Dahlstrom
Donna Chesnut, assistant

If you like this book, look for these other Simply Handmade™ titles wherever quality books are sold.

Or visit our website at bhgbooks.com

Fulfill your passion for making handcrafted gifts and decorations with this inspirational book. You'll find hundreds of creative new ways to make treasures for every day of the year.

Celebrate special events and holidays with wonderful projects you craft yourself. No matter if you have a minute, an evening, or a weekend, you'll always have a marvelous craft idea on hand.

A gift from the kitchen is sure to bring smiles. Wrap it beautifully and it will be remembered and treasured. This book offers delicious recipes and extraordinary gift wraps that combine for grand presentations.